Critical Nuclear War Survival Skills Guide

Essential Tactics and Strategies for
Immediate Family Safety and Security in a
Post-Apocalyptic World

Carlos Mack

Table of Contents

JUST FOR YOU!

As a way of saying **THANK YOU** for your purchase, I'm offering you these 2 FREE bonus gifts exclusive to my readers!

FREE bonus #1: 10 Essential Home Remedy Supplies For Preppers

FREE bonus #2: 20 Hygiene Products That All Preppers Should Store

To receive your 2 FREE bonus gifts scan the QR code below:

SCAN ME

Introduction

If you have ever heard of nuclear war, then you know it is something that has the potential to cause immense destruction and a catastrophic loss of life. Though nuclear war may feel like a far distant nightmare, it is something that is actually a genuine threat right now—one we must acknowledge, and one we must prepare for.

Have we ever been close to this destruction before? We have, but we avoided it because of the rational decision made by one man.

This catastrophic outcome almost befell us during the Cuban Missile Crisis in 1962. This was amid the Cold War, and the tensions between the United States and the Soviet Union were at an all-time high. The Soviets had been building missiles on the island of Cuba, which was just miles away from the US mainland. The US had to respond, and they did so by placing a naval blockade around Cuba. For the next several days, the tense situation teetered on the edge of nuclear war. The world was on the razor's edge, and its fate rested in the hands of just a few individuals.

Cooler heads had to prevail, and one of those "cooler heads" was Vasili Arkhipov. Arkhipov was part of a Soviet submarine fleet that was approaching the US blockade. While the rest of the fleet kept a safe distance, one submarine ventured too close and had been spotted. American destroyer ships surrounded the sub and forced it to go underwater. The US naval fleet deployed practice depth charges in order to get the submarine to surface.

Because of the charges going off and the conditions on the submarine after days underwater, its captain figured that the war had already broken out. He wanted to launch a torpedo at an American destroyer ship, but these weren't regular torpedoes. This naval fleet was all carrying a torpedo fitted with a nuclear warhead. If they were attacked or just felt that war had begun, they were tasked to fire.

But since this was a dangerous payload that would have grave consequences if fired, the Soviets had to get approval from the other captain of the fleet. That captain was Arkhipov. While the submerged ship was calling to launch its torpedo, Arkhipov was convinced that the US was only doing this to raise the submarine to the surface. Therefore, he refused to give the go-ahead. This simple but brave decision prevented a global nuclear war, saving the world from utter destruction.

The story of Arkhipov is one that highlights how important it is for us to understand nuclear war. It's also important to understand and be prepared for its potential occurrence. And this brings us to the contents of this book.

At the time of writing, we are moving through the year 2023. It is a time when the world's political climate is more uncertain and volatile than it has ever been. The ongoing conflict between Russia and Ukraine continues to escalate. The longer the conflict goes on, the more countries become involved, which only threatens to see this war spill outside of that localized region. Meanwhile, there are ongoing tensions the United States has with North Korea. Both sides have taken provocative actions that could eventually lead to a nuclear conflict between the countries. Then, we have China's growing military prowess and territorial ambitions that have caused concern to neighboring countries.

And what do we see as a response? Politicians and madmen across the globe who seem to care less and less about what happens to the world and its people. Instead, they are prioritizing their own interests. Their ambitions are driving us closer to that nuclear threat.

You probably have questions of your own, like how can you protect yourself and your family if the worst happens? What supplies do you need? How can you get your home ready? Do you need to leave your home? Are you or your family going to be facing any emotional and psychological challenges because of nuclear war?

There is a lot to take in, but you have to be like that courageous submarine captain—cool, calm, and ready for anything.

With the ever-present threat of a nuclear war hovering above our heads, it is becoming imperative that we do what we can to prepare for and survive the worst-case scenario. Throughout this book, we will look at all those steps to get you ready to keep yourself and your loved ones safe. I will also provide you with a deeper insight into nuclear weapons—where they started, how they advanced, and who has them right now.

After you know the history of these powerful weapons, then I will start providing you with the survival skills that might save your life before, during, and after the bombs fall. With 15 years of prepper experience, I can tell you that you don't want to wait for disaster to strike to do something. This book will arm you with the knowledge and skills you need to know to survive a nuclear war.

Stay vigilant, stay prepared!

Chapter 1:

Understanding the Threat of

Nuclear War

Mr. President, we and you ought not now to pull off the ends of the rope in which you have tied the knot of war, because the more the two of us pull, the tighter that knot will be tied. And a moment may come when that knot will be tied so tight that even he who tied it will not have the strength to untie it, and then it will be necessary to cut that knot, and what that would mean is not for me to explain to you, because you yourself understand perfectly of what terrible forces our countries dispose.

That was part of one correspondence from Soviet leader Nikita Krushchev to American president John F. Kennedy during the Cuban Missile Crisis. The former sent this telegram to the latter on October 26th, 1962, which was one day before Arkhipov made his courageous decision.

This first chapter will provide a comprehensive history of nuclear weapons, including the different weapons and their delivery systems. While that will help to a degree, you will have a better understanding of this threat by knowing what the current state of it is. It is absolutely crucial to understand the magnitude of a nuclear war if you want to prepare for it.

The best place to start is at the beginning and work our way to the nuclear landscape of today.

History of Nuclear Weapons

Manhattan Project

In 1939, United States intelligence teams received word that German scientists were working on the development of a nuclear weapon. President Franklin D. Roosevelt would set up the Advisory Committee on Uranium, which aimed to research uranium as a potential weapon. Enrico Fermi and Leo Szilard would work on uranium enrichment, but overall the research and development would move slowly—largely because the US was not involved in World War II. By 1941, we would know the committee as the Office of Scientific Research and Development (OSRD), which Fermi was part of.

In December 1941, the United States would be forced into the war after the Japanese attack on Pearl Harbor, and the development process of an atomic weapon would be pushed into overdrive.

The Army Corps of Engineers would join the OSRD in 1942, and development would become a military initiative. This led to the development of the Manhattan Engineer District with Colonel Leslie Groves at the helm. Meanwhile, Fermi and Szilard had finally produced the enriched uranium needed for a nuclear weapon. By the end of the year, President Roosevelt would authorize the establishment of laboratories and facilities all over the country that would work together to develop an atomic bomb.

At the heart of this effort was the Los Alamos Laboratory in New Mexico under the leadership of J. Robert Oppenheimer, which was established in 1943. Los Alamos—known as Project Y—would be the location that would take everyone else's work to assemble the bomb. Los Alamos would come up with two designs: the Little Boy, which used enriched uranium, and the Fat Man, which used plutonium.

The bombs would be ready in 1945, but a test needed to be done with the plutonium design. So, in the White Sands region of New Mexico, on July 16th, 1945, the Trinity Test was run, and the first atomic bomb in the world was detonated.

The Bombings of Hiroshima and Nagasaki

The development of atomic weaponry was done out of fear that Germany would build theirs first and use it in the war. However, by the time the Trinity Test happened, Germany had already surrendered. Later findings would show that they had long abandoned their atomic programs to focus on the war. However, the United States' fight with Japan was still raging on.

It was a back-and-forth war with no sign of either side willing to back down. While Japan would get in deadly attacks on America, they were usually fighting from the ropes. Around the same time as the Trinity Test, Japan had refused another demand for their surrender—a move that prompted Allied forces to threaten utter destruction.

The proposed response from America (initially) was a large-scale invasion, which was shot down on account it would risk too many Allied lives. Talks then turned toward using the newfound atomic power, which left another debate on the table about where the bomb should be detonated.

Thinking that using the bomb would finally force Japan to surrender and end the war, the manufacturing center, Hiroshima, was chosen as a target. On the morning of August 6th, 1945, the Enola Gay would drop the 9,000-pound uranium bomb over the city. The Little Boy detonated approximately 2,000 feet over the city, which leveled five square miles of Hiroshima.

Japan still refused to surrender, so three days later, the plutonium bomb (Fat Man) was dropped over the city of Nagasaki. Finally, Emperor Hirohito announced the unconditional surrender, which sealed the end of World War II. Between both bombs, about 130,000 to 215,000 people died in the two Japanese cities. Those deaths include those who were in the immediate vicinity and those who suffered acute exposure and long-term side effects. Because of the last factor, the exact death toll is unknown.

The Hydrogen Bomb (Cold War)

The global shakeup didn't stop with the bombings in Japan. The Soviet Union had been an ally during World War II, but after the war, they were viewed as a threat. Other governments felt the Soviets would start making the same push that Nazi Germany had made, so the United States employed a containment strategy.

The containment strategy would see America build up its armament and encourage the development of more weapons like the ones used at the end of the war. The Soviets weren't quiet during this time, though. In 1949, they tested an atomic bomb of their own, which showed they were building up their own arms supply; thus kicking off what we know as the Cold War.

One development made by the US had been mentioned during the atomic bomb's infancy. Someone had proposed a "superbomb," which would use hydrogen in the core to speed up and intensify the chain reaction needed for detonation. Now that the defense budget increased, that bomb could be developed.

The true power—and genuine fear—of the atomic age was unleashed on November 1st, 1952, when the US tested the first thermonuclear (hydrogen) bomb in the Marshall Islands. The bomb would create an enormous fireball that vaporized an entire island and left a hole in the ocean floor.

What ensued after was each country developing more powerful bombs and testing them. The Soviet Union detonated the most powerful of these thermonuclear bombs in 1961. The Tsar Bomba detonated over the Mityushikha Bay, and the world would get a glimpse at just how far development could be pushed.

The flare from the Tsar Bomba was seen as far away as Norway, Greenland, and Alaska. Its blast and seismic waves circled the Earth three times, and it shattered windows in places over 400 miles from the detonation site.

The Cuban Missile Crisis

While the United States was still trying to stockpile arms and nuclear weapons against Russia, an additional threat emerged from the south. Fidel Castro and his revolutionaries led a revolt in Cuba and succeeded in overthrowing the former government. One of the first things that Castro did was side with the Soviet Union, which now put the potential Soviet threat closer to home.

Matters were not made any better in April 1961, when America would attempt a Cuban invasion at the Bay of Pigs. Because of this failed attempt, all matters had to be handled delicately with the communist island and its allies.

While we already went over the most important parts of the Cuban Missile Crisis, it is worth noting again how close the world came to being under a blanket of nuclear fallout. Not only did Arkhipov keep his calm in a tense moment, but President Kennedy would also not give in to the pressures of his advisors to retaliate against Cuba after they had shot down the plane of Rudolf Anderson, killing the American pilot.

The immediate threat of nuclear war was gone after the crisis as a new direct line between D.C. and Moscow was put in place to aid in de-escalating future situations. Despite this and the treaties signed by the countries, the arms race continued as the Soviets now turned their attention to intercontinental ballistic missiles.

The Nuclear Treaties

The arms race between the United States and the Soviet Union was now spreading across the world. In 1970, the Treaty on the Non-Proliferation of Nuclear Weapons would authorize five nations (the US, the USSR, China, France, and the United Kingdom) to have nuclear weapons—no questions asked.

We were now deep in the atomic age, and the number of nuclear warheads would continue to rise. By 1986, there were 70,000 missile-mounted warheads in various places around the world. For context, global devastation could be guaranteed with the detonation of under 100 thermonuclear bombs.

In 1987, the Intermediate-Range Nuclear Forces Treaty (INF) was made between the United States and the Soviet Union. Much like the name suggests, this treaty was intended to eliminate the "medium-range" missiles that both countries possessed. For the first time since their invention, there would be a decline in the number of nuclear weapons.

There was also the Strategic Arms Reduction Talks that were happening in the 1980s. These talks were significant because they forced the nuclear nations to disclose how many nuclear arms they had on hand. Between these talks and the INF, the number of warheads dropped from that 70,000 mark. By 2021, there were only around 13,000 warheads in the world.

The last significant treaty was implemented in 2021. Countries around the world that signed the treaty agreed they would not develop, test, produce, stockpile, station, transfer, use, or threaten to use nuclear weapons.

It would be great to think that these treaties, talks, and agreements cleanly handled the issue of nuclear weapons, putting the matter to bed. However, not everyone agreed to those treaties, and even countries that agreed have found themselves no longer complying. While we should look at the nuclear nations, let's first start with what types of bombs exist out there—and their effects.

Types of Nuclear Weapons and Their Effects

Atomic Bomb

The atomic bomb, also known as the atom bomb or the A-bomb, is a fission weapon that uses a pure fission reaction to create an explosive yield of between 1 ton and 500 kilotons of TNT. It's the same type of bomb that was used over Hiroshima and Nagasaki, which had a yield between 15 and 20 kilotons of TNT. Most nuclear nations that begin producing weapons are going to start with this type of bomb because it's less demanding technically than other bomb designs.

To make the bomb work, it needs a fission reaction, which is where a neutron is launched at a high rate of speed into a larger atom to make it split in two. When there is a successful split, energy and more neutrons are released. These neutrons are then launched into larger atoms, causing them to split. The process then repeats until detonation.

As you read earlier, the materials used in atomic bombs are typically enriched uranium or plutonium because they are easier to control, and it is easier to initiate the chain reaction. The methods used to start that reaction are the gun type and the implosion, with the implosion method being the more efficient of the two.

One of the major issues with the atomic bomb is all the material in that core isn't used. There is an abundance of highly radioactive and moderately radioactive fission products. The highly radioactive products are terrifying, but they will dissipate faster. The moderately radioactive products, though, are long-lived. Both types of fission products, though, are what are responsible for nuclear fallout.

Thermonuclear Bomb

Fusion bombs, otherwise known as hydrogen bombs (H-bombs) or thermonuclear bombs, are the superbombs that were proposed well before the completion of the first atomic weapons. While these bombs pack a devastating punch and are highly efficient, they still take much more skill to construct. However, almost all the nuclear weapons in deployment at this very moment are all a thermonuclear design.

As the name "fusion" suggests, this needs a fusion reaction to work. Fusion reactions are when two atoms collide to form a heavier atom. Our best example of this is what keeps our sun burning bright. Two hydrogen atoms collide to form helium—and a lot of energy. However, this is very hard to do on our own planet. The amount of pressure and heat needed to fuse two atoms together is extremely high, so it has to be done in shorter bursts, which requires another stage made of a fission reaction.

Most thermonuclear weapons use a two-stage design where the fission reaction is set off, which then compresses and heats a fusion fuel (tritium, deuterium, or lithium deuteride). The fusion reaction will finish producing the energy seen during the explosion.

While a pure fusion bomb would virtually eliminate fission products, fusion materials are difficult to control, so there is typically a fission stage in place. Because of that, thermonuclear bombs can produce as much fallout as a fission bomb. The problem with that lies in how powerful these bombs are. When they explode, they will launch debris—often with radioactive particles mixed in—into the atmosphere that can settle hundreds of miles away from the point of impact.

Dirty Bomb

Dirty bombs are going to be linked more to terrorist weaponry. While they have the potential to cause severe harm and death, their main purpose is to cause widespread panic. There has yet to be a dirty bomb attack on record, which is likely because of the extreme difficulty with acquiring nuclear materials.

The technical name for a dirty bomb is a "radiological dispersion device." Its name is just as it sounds; this is a conventional bomb with radioactive material inside. Dirty bombs will use dynamite or other easy-to-make explosion methods, and then there will be a variety of materials, including radioactive materials around them. When the bomb explodes, shrapnel and the radioactive material is launched outward.

While it is easy *and* cheaper to make, the problem is with coming up with a sufficient amount of radioactive material. The maker of the bomb can try to get medical or industrial materials, or they can take it from a research facility. However, those materials are under more security because of their radioactivity.

There is the potential that the bomb maker can find black market materials, but even if there were nuclear materials for sale, they are going to be bought by manufacturers of more sophisticated weapons.

Again, this is a terrorist weapon meant to cause massive panic, and there indeed would be if one was ever detonated. There would be a loss of life in the explosion's vicinity, but it's unlikely a person would get sick with radiation poisoning after a dirty bomb explosion. With that being said, the real threat of a dirty bomb comes from a nuclear nation using a dirty bomb to frame another country for a terrorist attack.

The Effects of Nuclear Bombs

Direct radiation: This is the first effect of a nuclear blast, where there will be a large burst of radiation, primarily made of gamma rays and neutrons. Direct radiation is not the major cause for concern, though, with everything else happening at the same time.

Fireball: At the moment of detonation, the bomb itself is vaporized because the energy released is hotter than the core of the sun. The hot gas emitted will heat the air around the explosion, which will form a fireball. The heat within this fireball causes it to glow brighter than the sun for up to 50 miles away.

Thermal flash: As the air is heating and a glowing fireball is made, there is that initial bright flash that makes up one-third of the energy in the bomb. The heat here is so intense that it can start fires and cause severe burns to people even 20 miles away.

Blast wave: As the fireball climbs into the sky, there is an abrupt spike in air pressure, which creates the blast wave that moves outwardly, starting at thousands of miles per hour. Most of the physical destruction from a nuclear bomb comes from the blast wave that creates overpressure. To explain overpressure: there is a force all around you. This force is around 15 pounds per square inch (psi), but you can't feel it because it's always been there. During a nuclear blast, there is going to be far more air pressure on one side of an object with nothing to counter it. The pressure itself can be so strong that it can throw you great distances, and though most people can survive this, they are more at risk now of buildings falling on them.

Firestorm: After the blast wave passes through, there is still more destruction to come. The fires that started when the bomb detonated are still burning strong, and sometimes they will come together as one enormous blaze, which causes a firestorm. Firestorms can generate their own winds, and that will cause the fires to spread. As the hot gasses rise, they are replaced by air rushing in at an alarming rate of speed. What is left is an environment without oxygen, and this can suffocate anyone in the area. Firestorms will also have a long-lasting effect on the Earth's atmosphere.

Fallout: Those fission products that I mentioned earlier are what will make up the nuclear fallout that will fall long after the immediate effects of the bomb are over. Fallout can be dangerous as it can be carried to areas outside of the initial bomb radius. The amount of fallout that is sent out depends on where the bomb was detonated (ground or air bursts). While fallout can spread for miles and last for years after a bombing, the most lethal effects are the first few days or weeks afterward.

Variables

There are going to be variables with nuclear bombs, which will affect everything we have just gone over. To lead off, we will start with the biggest variable: air burst versus ground burst.

- An air burst is going to see the weapon detonating thousands of feet over the target. Widespread physical damage to an area is going to come from an air burst. Densely populated areas and areas with a government (non-military) presence would be the targets of an air burst.

- Ground bursts will detonate upon impact with the ground, which will destroy everything in close range, but the other blast effects are kept to a minimum. Significant military targets, especially areas underground, will be the target of ground burst attacks.

One thing that will change is the nuclear fallout from the bombs. With an air burst, more fallout is released into the stratosphere. This can carry fallout across the globe. With a ground burst, there is a tremendous amount of nuclear material attached to dirt and rocks that are launched into the air. Larger particles will rain back down, which can create radioactive "hot spots." Smaller particles can be carried, but not as far.

Of course, the size of the bomb will make an enormous difference. The larger the bomb, the wider the blast radius is. But as the bombings in Japan would show us, the targeted location makes an enormous difference. The bomb that fell over Nagasaki should have had greater or equal effects, but it was far tamer because of the rough terrain. Of the two bombs, Hiroshima was the only one that produced a firestorm.

Nuclear Weapon Delivery Systems

Nuclear bombs can come in a variety of sizes, which means they need different methods of delivery, which is where the nuclear triad comes in. The nuclear triad is used by all nuclear nations, and it is a combination of land-launched nuclear missiles (ICBMs), submarines with missiles (SLBMs), and strategic bombers that can have both nuclear bombs and missiles.

It may seem like a lot of methods, but they are necessary. In the event of an attack, countries can't risk all of their nuclear arms being destroyed on the first strike. So, by having three different delivery systems, a country will at least have a chance to retaliate. The goal is not to just launch a counterattack; the triad is put in place to deter nations from even launching a first strike.

Strategic Bombers

These are typically the first leg of the nuclear triad because of their flexibility with how they are deployed and what they can carry. They are also the first leg because they can be deployed and recalled in an instant. Because they can be recalled and sent away from targets, their deployment can be seen as a country wanting to negotiate instead of fight.

Their flexibility in payload, though, can be a slight problem. While modern warfare allows aircraft to be hidden on radar, they can still be spotted with the human eye. Upon detection, a country could assume the plane is carrying a nuclear payload, even when they aren't, which can trigger a counterattack.

Intercontinental Ballistic Missiles (ICBMs)

When a country wants to execute a long-range strike from a remote area, it will probably be using an ICBM. These missiles can launch and reach targets faster than the other methods, and they are the definitive sign a nation is engaging in nuclear warfare. ICBMs can either be launched from fixed positions such as missile silos, or they can be moved around by rail lines or conventional roads.

One problem with ICBMs would be with the fixed position method. Intelligence obtained by other countries will highlight a nation's missile silos; making them a primary target in an attack. Of course, the other disadvantage comes from the "shoot first, ask questions later" aspect of the bomb. Once they are fired, there is little to no chance of that missile being recalled, which will spark an all-out nuclear assault.

There are also medium-range ballistic missiles and cruise missiles that can be launched from the ground, but these were forbidden during one treaty between the United States and Russia.

Submarine-Launched Ballistic Missiles (SLBMs)

With low detectability, mobility, and ability to remain undetectable, SLBMs are a perfect second-wave attack in the event of a nuclear war. Because of the method of deployment, it is difficult to get a location to return fire.

The things that make SLBMs great are also what can lead to their problems. Because a missile loaded on a submarine can still explode, this can lead to problems determining if it was an attack or an operational error. Also, the costs to maintain a submarine carrying this type of payload, along with the size of crew needed and the patrol ships needed to protect it can become astronomical for one sub alone—let alone a fleet of them.

Nonstrategic Weapons

There are certainly more types of nuclear weapons, and those would be considered tactical nukes that can be used through air, land, and sea delivery. Their primary uses are going to be in the face of battle—more localized weaponry, but depending on the technology used and the target, these could also be a part of the triad.

Different missions are going to call for certain methods, and weapons in the triad might be too large-scale. Air-to-air missiles, surface-to-air missiles, rockets, bombs, land mines, demolition charges, artillery shells, vehicle-mounted rifles, and even munitions can all be fitted with nuclear warheads. By using nonstrategic weapons, a nation can send counterattacks or station them in places for a fraction of the cost.

An example of this would be submarines. While there will be subs with strategic weapons, there are more with depth charges, torpedoes, rockets, and gunnery shells.

The State of Nuclear Threats

As you learned earlier, the nuclear treaties and disarmament talks would only make nine nuclear nations. So, who are they and how many weapons do they have? What advances in warfare (regular and nuclear) have they made? Are there any outside nations looking to buy nuclear weapons or materials on the black market? How many of these treaties have eroded because of the increasing tensions in the world?

All the numbers here are approximate, and the exact amount is always changing.

The Nuclear Nations

- The United States: 5,200 total, 1,600 strategically deployed, 100 nonstrategically deployed, triad nation

- Russia: 6,000 total, 1,700 strategically deployed, triad nation

- France: 300 total, 250 strategically deployed, former triad nation

- China: 400 total, none deployed, triad nation

- United Kingdom: 225 total, 120 strategically deployed

- Israel: 90 total, none deployed, suspected triad nation

- Pakistan: 170 total, none deployed

- India: 164 total, none deployed, triad nation

- North Korea: 30 total, none deployed

One of the biggest problems with the number of arms is that countries have become less transparent about how many they have. The same could be said about the next section as well.

Advances in Warfare

A misconception about modern nuclear weapons is that they are far more powerful than anything we saw tested during the Cold War. That simply isn't true, but that doesn't make them any less dangerous.

With the advancements in technology, we now have far more accurate GPS tracking. Satellite imagery can send those images back in real-time, exposing the location of active targets. So, when thinking about using nuclear weapons, the more accurate a country can be with its strikes, the more efficient they are with the weapons they do have. Think of having several nuclear missiles hitting their targets in several moderate explosions as opposed to having one extremely large explosion that is miles off target.

Not that a country doesn't have the means to make an extremely large bomb. Most of them could, but those bombs are inefficient and difficult to carry. Also, going back to radar and tracking technology, large bomber planes are easy to see on radar and with the naked eye, which allows room for a counterattack.

The Nuclear Black Market

For the most part, the nuclear nations wouldn't openly sell their weapons, and most of them wouldn't want to part with their stockpiles, anyway. However, what happens if materials or weapons are stolen and sold to the highest bidder? What about the countries that are willing to make a deal with a terrorist nation? That's where the black market comes into play.

Since the Cold War, there has always been a place on the black market for nuclear materials. Weapons are much harder to sell and move around, but materials will help anyone looking to get some advantage in warfare. Fortunately, the materials that make it on the black market are not enough to cause any significant harm. They would likely be used for dirty bombs.

And yes, it happens more often than you think. In 2021, Indian police arrested several individuals and confiscated a few kilograms of pure uranium that they were trying to sell on the black market. This raises questions about the security around these materials, too, as large quantities of uranium in India have gone missing.

It's also not just the start-up nuclear nations that have issues with materials being stolen. The United States lost six nuclear weapons during the Cold War, and since 2010, there have been two instances where nuclear materials have gone missing. In 2018, a car had been broken into in Texas, and among the contents stolen were plutonium and cesium. Then, in July 2021, materials on their way to Michigan would be misplaced. In this instance, the materials were found, but what is alarming is the frequency with which materials are getting misplaced.

The State of Nuclear Treaties

Treaties are signed, agreements are made, and talks happen all the time. This is just part of the political ebb and flow that happens all over the world. This means that it's only natural that after a certain amount of time new tensions will shake up the political landscape.

One country that has put other nations on edge is North Korea. There have been unauthorized missile tests and threats from the country. It has prompted responses from other nations, with calls to retaliate against North Korea, but it has also prompted talks from neighboring South Korea. With the threat of North Korea invading again, many in South Korea feel that their best response might be to have nuclear weapons of their own.

Now, we can look at the prominent nuclear powers—Russia and the United States. These are perfect examples of how tensions can affect established treaties. As the war in Ukraine heated up, there were more talks from Russian President Vladimir Putin about using nuclear weapons as retaliation if any country got involved in the war.

Another sign that Russia was serious about using nuclear weapons happened in February 2023, when the country suspended the only nuclear treaty it had with the United States. They would later clarify that Russia intended to follow the caps set on nuclear weapons and they would still exchange information about ballistic missile tests. What increases the tension is that the treaty would call for regular inspections of nuclear sites.

Both the United States and Russia also pulled out of the Intermediate-Range Nuclear Forces Treaty that had been signed in 1987. This happened in 2017 and was caused when the US suspected Russia of using a new type of cruise missile that violated the treaty—something that Russia denied. However, it is important to note that even suspicions can lead to treaties being dissolved.

The state of the world today is one of suspicion, tension, and advancements in nuclear technology. While we should still look to the skies for bomber planes, the real threat is those missiles that can cross oceans—the missiles that are strategically deployed and aimed at very specific targets. If tensions grow, we could very well end up back in a situation like the Cuban Missile Crisis. The exception here is going to be how volatile these political parties are now. Who knows if they can remain calm and maintain civility while under pressure. But with this, you know what you're up against, which is the first step in prepping.

Chapter 2:

Preparing for Nuclear War

I know not with what weapons World War III will be fought, but World War IV will be fought with sticks and stones. –Albert Einstein

Now that you know who and what the threats are, you can start making the steps to getting yourself and your family prepared. Prepping for something that hasn't been weaponized in almost 80 years can be a little daunting, but you can get there as long as you know what you need to do to prepare.

You need to find or create your own shelter, but more than that, you have to make sure that this shelter is stockpiled to last you for a while. And while it would be great if you could just get in your shelter and wait out the bombs, there is always the possibility that an attack will happen when you least expect it, which means you will be far away from home. Having an emergency plan and a backup plan are essential. So, this is a must-read chapter if you want to be proactive in prepping against nuclear war.

Shelter for Nuclear Survival

Bomb Shelter vs Fallout Shelter

If you've ever had an inkling of nuclear war, you know that there was probably the mention of a fallout shelter or a bomb shelter. You might think they are the same thing, but they are two very different structures, and they are both going to serve a unique purpose.

A bomb shelter is going to be ideal for those who are living within a 30-mile radius of a major city. Depending on the type of bomb used and where it detonates, a bomb shelter can withstand the initial blast and effects of a nuclear bomb. While this can be a plausible idea, a bomb shelter would need to be placed underground, which makes the cost of the structure astronomical for just one person. If you are this close to a major city, I would recommend either bugging out or searching for a bomb shelter in the area.

A fallout shelter is going to be much better suited for those farther away from those major cities. With a fallout shelter, you can build an above-ground shelter for a tiny fraction of what a bomb shelter would cost. You could make a small cinder block structure, install an air purification system, and stack sandbags around it, which altogether isn't expensive and will protect you from any waves of radiation and fallout that may rain down.

Again, you only want to go underground if you are closer to places that seem like first strike targets, or if you have money to burn.

Key Factors When Considering a Fallout Shelter

When building or even buying something that you will use as a fallout shelter, there are certain aspects that you need to look at ahead of time.

Safety and comfort: Above everything else, you want to be somewhere that won't leave you exposed to waves of radiation or radioactive fallout, and you need to plan to have an entrance and emergency exit. Afterward, you should think about having something that gets the maximum amount of comfort that you can get. It's not going to be luxurious, but you want to make sure there is plenty of space to move around, lie down, and handle any business, like using the restroom.

Ventilation: Ventilation will provide fresh air to the structure, which can quickly feel stuffy when at full occupancy. This is where you want to take more precautions, though, because while you can install a DIY ventilation system, you need to make sure it is still filtering out any particles that may be radioactive.

Cost-effective: It can be really tempting to start spending money on a fallout shelter. You can avoid breaking the bank if you just remember to be practical. This shelter is only there to get you through the initial period after the blasts. Keep in mind that you can still buy quality reinforced materials while keeping costs low.

Waste management: Sometimes an overlooked aspect of a shelter is going to be where the inhabitants can use the restroom. There should be a space designated, and it should be in a place where the smell is being vented out. This is especially important during the initial period after the blasts when you should not venture out.

Fire extinguishers and first aid: Even if your shelter is safe on the outside, is it safe on the inside? This is where you and your loved ones are, so you should make sure you have the same fire-preventative measures in place that you have in the home. While you should have a bug out bag with you, this space should still have extra first aid supplies in case something happens when making your way to the shelter.

Food and water storage: Besides the room you need to make for everything listed above and the inhabitants of the shelter, you should have plenty of food and water just in case you do need to have an extended stay here.

Building Materials and Techniques for a Successful Shelter

This section is going to give you several ideas that you can use on your own property. Some of you will have plenty of space for a shipping container, but there will be those who are going to be limited by state and local regulations—not to mention homeowners associations. For those areas, you might have to think on a smaller scale to something a little more spartan. However, no matter what shelter you decide on, you are going to significantly increase your survival odds if your shelter is solid.

Shipping Containers

Shipping containers are becoming more and more popular for things like building homes and other structures, which begs the question: can be used for a fallout shelter?

Remember to think about where you are in relation to potential nuclear targets. If you are far enough away from what could be an impact point, then a shipping container will be a great shelter. Fallout cannot get through, and any fallout that reaches the area has either already lost—or will quickly lose—its radioactive potency. Some things to keep in mind, though, if choosing this as your shelter, are the following:

- The flooring in a shipping container is sealed with toxic chemicals, so you will need to install new flooring and seal off the rest of the chemicals.

- You will need to reinforce the structure to ensure that it will last for years to come. This includes reinforcing the frame and waterproofing the container so it doesn't rot through and leak.

Granted, you might be closer to a potential target, so now you have to think about those waves of radiation that can penetrate the walls of a shipping container. This might leave you thinking of taking your shipping container and burying it to make an effective bomb shelter. This is feasible and it will give you a shelter that is close to military-grade, but it is going to become a very lengthy and expensive process. You are probably better off looking toward other building materials and designs, but if this is still the best route for you, then keep these things in mind:

- Shipping containers were never meant to be buried, and they can't withstand the constant pressure of being buried that far below ground. You still have to reinforce the inside of the frame, but now you have to do the same to the outside of the container.

- You can't do partial burials. Your container has to have approximately three to six feet of dirt covering it to keep radiation out of the container. Most areas that would be closer to impact sites will not allow that kind of digging on your property. So, if you are thinking about a bomb shelter, you should find more cost-effective and practical methods.

Concrete or Steel Structures

The idea here is similar to an outdoor tornado shelter. One of the most positive aspects is that these structures are reinforced, so you can be a little closer to impact sites. It's a perfect idea for those suburban areas, and they can be above-ground or partially buried.

The downside to these shelters is if you are purchasing them, they are relatively small, which makes them only good for short-term stays. Don't rule them out, though. Just keep in mind that if you use one of these shelters, you will need to have an immediate backup plan.

This method also gives you a way to build your own shelter from cinder blocks that are surrounded by three feet of sandbags around it. As long as there is an air filtration system in place, an entrance, and an emergency exit, this DIY shelter will work for most people.

There should not be windows or exposed wood on the shelter. Blast waves will shatter windows and the thermal energy can easily ignite wood in areas that are in proximity to where the bomb detonated.

Earthbag Shelter

Earthbag shelters are great shelters to build, although they can take a lot of labor hours to construct. Once you cover the outside with a layer of plaster, you have an attractive structure that can shield you from any radiation waves and fallout particles. This method is usually used by the military in emergency situations, and it is also a construction method used in areas with a lot of natural disasters.

This is one of the methods that I would certainly suggest. You can start with a smaller structure, and then work your way up to something that will allow plenty of room for everyone who will be in there. You have this type of flexibility because of how inexpensive these are to build, not to mention how easy they are to build.

Earthbag shelters can stand up to a lot, including what you're preparing for here. The only thing to remember is to avoid using anything wooden around the outside of the structure. If anything, the door frame and anything else should be made from steel.

Geodesic Shelter

Much like earthbag shelters, geodesic domes are becoming more popular in the prepper community. These domes are made from an array of triangles that form the half-sphere, and they can cover the most space with the least materials. So, what else is making these structures as popular as they are?

They are strong, and that strength is chalked up to the triangles that make up the structure. Triangles can take pressure from one edge and place it on the other two sides. When you add more of them, you get a self-supporting structure. Because it is self-supporting, you have more space under the dome. More space is great for maintaining an even temperature and promoting air circulation. This also makes it effective against powerful winds and other storms, which would be great against blast waves, too.

However, with the materials that are typically used, it is imperative that you have a way to get coverage from radiation waves. Again, fallout is scary, but you're mostly protected in any structure. Those initial waves that can stretch out, though, call for a thicker barrier between them and you.

Converted Basement Shelter

This is the most common and cheapest fallout shelter—and can potentially act as a bomb shelter too. It typically has enough room for everyone in the home with plenty of space to stockpile supplies. Most basements even have a ground-level window for ventilation, and some basements will have two entry points.

These are a great idea, but you still need to be prepared to put in some work to make sure it's nuclear-ready. The first thing is replacing your doors. The hollow door leading into your basement from the home should definitely be replaced. Doors leading outside are typically heavy and solid, but you want to replace these, too. Just keep in mind that armor doors are going to be very expensive. But when you replace these doors, you can ensure that they are sealed properly.

If you have a window, you need to fit a sliding steel shutter on it. Again, make sure the area around is sealed. Before deeming it "ready," you want to make sure the rest of the room is reinforced, mainly your ceiling. In the event your home is leveled in a blast, you want to make sure it will not affect where you're hiding.

Reinforced Existing Rooms

What about the existing structures that are already on your property? There are those of you who have garages, sheds, and maybe even a barn, but can you use them for a fallout shelter?

You can, of course, as long as you reinforce and retrofit the structure to be ready for nuclear fallout. The only thing that should stop you from doing this work on an existing structure is if you are close to a potential target.

Expedient Shielding Materials

You might be put in a situation where you only have a limited time to make an expedient fallout shelter. You want something that will give you the same effect as four inches of concrete. We already covered the earthbags, which you can use to build your entire shelter, but these are the things you can use, as well:

- five to six inches of brick

- six inches of sand or gravel

- eight inches of hollow concrete

If you have access to any old books, you can make or line your shelter with 14 inches of books or magazines. 18 inches of wood will also work, which is why many bug out locations are log cabins. While these can be used to make an expedient shelter, you shouldn't hesitate to build. Best-case scenarios of a large-scale ICBM assault are only going to give you 30 minutes to get sheltered.

Expedient Shelter Options

There are other things you can use if you need to make a shelter in a hurry. Remember that these shelters are temporary, and you should always have plans to move to a permanent shelter after the bombings have subsided.

Under-Stair Shelter

A lot of stairways are at a central location of a home, and they have enough space that you can get into in a hurry. While this can be an expedient shelter, you can still plan ahead and add bricks, concrete blocks, or other materials around that space. Bookcases and storage racks can be placed under the stairs to add additional support.

If you are far enough away from potential targets, you can keep shielding materials close by, and when you get a warning, you can move quickly to get those materials in place.

If you don't have a stairway or a basement, you can even use a crawl space if your home has one. Remember, any distance and barrier you can get between you and nuclear fallout is a good thing.

Trench Shelter

This shelter is definitely an emergency situation, but it will work. With a shovel, dig a trench in the shape of an L. The long side of this trench will be the shelter itself, and the shorter side of the L will serve as the entrance. It is important that you make the best right angle that you can for the entrance because this will cut down on any radiation that may seep into the shelter.

Go to your emergency pack or where you have your supplies and grab your tarps or plastic sheets. If you have a large piece of plywood, this will help, too, as you need to construct a roof for the shelter. Lay the board down, followed by the sheeting material. Make sure you are leaving enough space for ventilation and an entrance. After you have those things in place, mound the earth that came from the trench over the top. This mound should be giving you at least two feet of shielding. You can also make earthbags to set on top of the shelter.

If you have the time and the materials, then you can line this trench with plywood or another shielding material. This will add more support to the sides, and you can lay a tarp on the floor of the trench to keep you from sitting on raw earth.

Expedient Car Shelter

If you are in your car when you get the alert that bombs are on the way, you can use your car as a shelter. As you're driving, look around for a trench that can fit under your car. Park over it, and your car is now your roof. If there is no trench, but you have a shovel in your car, you can dig an L-shaped trench and park your car over that.

Air Supply for Expedient Shelters

Again, if you are far enough away from the blast site, you don't need to have a complicated air filtration system. A wet bed sheet can be all you need to keep fallout particles out while still allowing breathable air in.

Stockpiling Supplies

After your shelter is constructed, stock it with supplies. As a prepper, supplies in your safe house or shelter are important, but they will be much more important when the disaster is nuclear war.

In the best-case scenario, you would be far enough away from everything and you can leave your shelter almost immediately—or at least walk around outside for a bit. However, we have to think about those scenarios that aren't ideal. You and your family could be in the shelter for a few days before you can reemerge. Worst-case scenarios could see you in there much longer.

Of course, one of your biggest considerations is going to be with space. Smaller shelters are going to be severely limited, which means you are going to need a detailed plan to move as soon as you can.

Water Storage

Water is one of the most important survival tools, but things are going to get very dicey in a nuclear war. Radiation waves and fallout particles are going to contaminate water sources, which will leave virtually all water undrinkable unless you can pull from deep wells, water tanks, seepage pits, or hand-dug wells. This is going to make water storage one of your more daunting tasks.

First, let's think about why you need water. Just by breathing, sweating, and having normal bodily functions, you are losing water. You have to replace it to stay properly hydrated. There's potential first aid that will require you to flush out wounds or clean off affected areas. Hygiene is also important in survival situations, so you'll need water to wash your hands and face, as well as brush your teeth.

Did you forget that you still have to cook your food? Grains and other items that you are going to store need water to be edible. With all of those uses, you're likely wondering now how much you need to store. At a minimum, you want a gallon a day per person, but even that is cutting it too close. I would suggest at least having two gallons per person for each day you plan on being in your shelter.

The challenge now is going to be what containers you are going to use, which is going to be at the mercy of the space you have to work with. The most common options are going to be bottled water, gallon jugs, five-gallon jugs, or large plastic drums. If you have the space, using a combination of methods will let you handle all your needs. But if you are struggling for room in your shelter, you might have to work with what makes sense for spacing and the water needs of everyone.

If you are using large containers like 55-gallon drums, you need to always be mindful of the safety of that water. Yes, you can pour it from your outside hose, but now you need to filter and purify that water.

- One of the simplest options for purifying water is to boil it before use. The issue here is that you might not have an area where you can make a fire. Even if you do, you can only boil small quantities before using it, and then you still have to wait until it cools.

- Another option is to use iodide or other chemical tablets to purify the water. There are several options out there that will take care of large drums, but the biggest problem here is the taste aspect.

There is still a way (space permitting) that you can use large containers or drums for all your water storage needs, however. Something like a Berkey water filter will filter out particles, and it will purify your water to make it safe for drinking. Given that you have a bug out vehicle, you can take your Berkey with you if your shelter is temporary. Possibly the largest drawback to this is needing to stock up on filters. Also, remember that these are great filters, but they will not work with water that is contaminated with radiation.

Food Storage

You want to build the perfect food storage, but, again, there are a lot of factors at work here. Those are factors that are going to be unique to you, and only you know what you have the ability to do. However, you're still going to want some direction about what you really need in your shelter.

- **Get things you already eat**: You want to get food items because they have a long shelf life or you're getting a good deal. But if you're not eating or using this food regularly, is it really going to fare well in your pantry? Of course, there are going to be sacrifices and diet changes, but items that aren't in your home should be a "last resort" item.

- **Long shelf life**: Rice, beans, and other grains are great things to stock given you have the means to cook them. However, it's easy to overlook canned foods that are ready to eat. Certain preservation methods are going to give some of these foods a very long shelf life.

- **Nutritional value**: Some comfort foods will be okay, especially for your mental well-being, but you don't want to stockpile "empty calories." With everything you are trying to do to survive, get foods high in nutrition and dense in calories.

- **Non-refrigerated foods**: When you are first hunkering down, you can live off some of your refrigerated foods so they won't go to waste. But it should go without saying—short shelf life and refrigerated foods shouldn't be in your stockpile.

- **Easy to prepare**: You're going to be cooking over a camping stove or a campfire, so you should make sure everything you do can be done with that method. Think of being as primitive as you can.

Now, you have to think about amounts. Account for how many people you will have in the shelter and how much food they are going to need per day. Then, you have to do a bit of guesswork by trying to determine how long you will be in the shelter. Making yourself a spreadsheet will be helpful when figuring out how much you need to buy, and it will come in handy when you are working through rotation, which we will come back to shortly.

After amounts, and before you buy anything, remember to adjust your lists for those with certain food allergies. So, what are key items most preppers will have in their storage?

- **Rice**: Rice is a great addition to any meal to achieve that full feeling. It can be served with almost any other food, and most people typically eat rice. But again, one of the best qualities of this is the very long shelf life.

- **Oatmeal**: This is another versatile food. It makes a great breakfast, and you can enhance the flavor with a bit of honey. You can also make snack foods from it depending on your other supplies.

- **Beans**: Beans are a great way to get protein, especially with meat becoming extremely scarce. They might not be everyone's favorite, but you can enhance the flavor profile with seasonings.

- **Canned meat**: Meat is still the best way to get protein, but hunting is almost ruled out in any areas close to the blast site. Even nuclear fallout will render meat inedible, so canned meats are not a bad idea.

  o If you or anyone in the shelter is a vegetarian, you can certainly look for foods that will provide that protein.

- **Canned fruit and vegetables**: These items won't last as long as grains or beans, but they can last you through a sizable chunk of shelter living. These will add much-needed vitamins and variety, and you can have meals that are closer to what you have now. While it may seem tempting to get the larger cans, I would suggest sticking to the smaller cans unless you have a large group.

- **Other items**: Honey is a great addition to add some comfort to a sweet snack, and it can last forever if stored properly. You're also going to need oils and fats, like vegetable oil, coconut oil, and peanut butter. Herbs and spices are good mostly to combat bland food, but one item you might have not thought of would be vitamins. A great multivitamin for everyone in the shelter will go a long way.

Maintaining a healthy, balanced diet is beneficial, so learning what everyone needs will help you plan effectively. When storing your food, you want to make sure it is proper storage, meaning that food is stored in sealed containers and never on the floor.

Emergency Gear and Miscellaneous Supplies

First Aid Kit

You are going to need a first aid kit for your bug out bag, and while this can double as your shelter's first-aid kit, I would recommend having a separate stockpile of first aid supplies in your shelter. The first thing you would need to work on is having an extra supply of important medications for you and your family. Talk to your pharmacist and doctor about how you can achieve this and how long those medications would be good for if stockpiled.

Another thing you will need in the event of nuclear war is iodine tablets or potassium iodide tablets. These tablets are being handed out in Ukraine, Poland, and other nations as Russia threatens nuclear attacks, as well as with how close battles have been to the Chernobyl plant. Radiation will affect your thyroid and cause cancer, but these tablets will slow those effects. These are going to be critical as you have to explore the outside world after an attack.

Ace bandages		Medical tape		OTC allergy medications	
Eye drops		Rolled gauze		Various sizes of bandaids, including butterfly bandages	
Safety pins		Moleskin		Ibuprofen	
Sterile latex gloves		Gauze pads		Medical shears	
Needle and thread		Syringes for wound irrigation		Antibiotics	
Thermometer		Aspirin		Hydrocortisone cream or sprays	
Tweezers		SAM splints		Pressure dressings	
Plastic cling wrap		Tourniquet		Acetaminophen	

Emergency blankets		Kelly clamps		Alcohol pads	
OPAs (keeps airways from closing)		N-95 masks		Antiseptics	
Dental filling		Cotton sheets		Floss	
Super glue		Eye pads		Antibiotic ointment and cream	
Dental extractors		Snake bite kit		Sutures	
CPR masks		Cervical collar		Epi-pen	
Variety of tapes (duct, adhesive, and paper tape)		Paracord		Eye cup	
Scalpels		QuikClot or Celox		Dental mirror	

Protective Gear and Clothes

As a survivalist, you want to be protected against the elements, but now you are trying to keep yourself safe from whatever radioactive particles are around. One of the best ideas here is having extra changes of clothes in your shelter for everyone. It should be something comfortable that can be layered to adjust for conditions.

For example, you want cooler clothes for the summer. But then you want to add items to shield yourself from the rain. When navigating the postnuclear world, you can use rain gear for its intended purpose or to protect yourself from fallout dust and other particles.

Another great addition for nuclear survival is going to be a heavy-duty mask with goggles. This will keep you from breathing in anything that could affect you later. You should also have plenty of disposable gloves and other items that can be gotten rid of after use.

Power and Lighting

In an ideal situation, you would have a generator in your shelter. You could also have solar panels or wind turbines for power, too. However, you can't rely solely on these means. You will need the things that you can take with you or use in case your major power sources are cut off.

One of the first is a heavy-duty power bank—preferably one that can be charged with solar power. A solid power bank can power flashlights, headlamps, and other small lights. It can also charge phones, radios, and other devices—in the event EMPs don't render those items useless.

You never want to be without lighters, matches, and extra batteries either. This will be especially true if you are in a shelter with no power where it can become dark easily. One of your best items here is going to be a hand-crank flashlight.

Overlooked Items and Items to Avoid

This doesn't apply to everyone, but you will have to account for infants and pets. Food, diapers, toys, and any special needs all need to be accounted for. After that, you want to make sure that you have everything you need for cooking. Those bags of rice and other items won't go far if you don't have any kitchenware.

But the most overlooked aspect of shelter supplies is for entertainment. Bring a deck of cards, board games, puzzles, and books. Of course, you should have age-appropriate items, especially for the smaller survivors.

When you are getting things moved to your shelter, or you're thinking about what you are going to take with you when there is an emergency, it's easy to start grabbing things that you don't need. Jewelry, cosmetics, gaming consoles, furniture, perfume—if it is not essential to your survival, it doesn't need to go with you. Priceless heirlooms and items of that nature should already be tucked away in a waterproof and fireproof box in your home or in your shelter.

Bug Out Bag (BOB)

In the event of *any* disaster, you should have one of these emergency packs ready to go for every member of your family. The contents of this bag are important, but the bag itself is also going to matter to you. This needs to be a heavy-duty, waterproof backpack that has plenty of space for everything you will need.

My recommendation is going to be a hiking backpack or a military tactical backpack. They will have everything that I just listed, but they will have more support and comfort so you can handle all the extra weight. It is best to go to an outdoor store to try on several different packs to find a bag that fits everyone comfortably. To pack the right contents, prep this bag for three days. This gives you and your family time to find a safer place to go, especially if you were closer to a nuclear strike. The following is a quick rundown of those "must-have items."

- **First aid kit**: Again, you should have a stockpile in your shelter, which can help you replenish the kits that go in your BOBs. The BOB first aid kit should have these items. Of course, things will change with the size of your pack, the space you have left, and the size of the first aid kit.

- **Water container (with filtration and purification)**: Water that isn't contaminated is going to be hard to find, but you should always be ready for when you do. For instance, if you come across a sealed well, this water just needs to be purified and filtered. I would recommend a Lifestraw, which can handle both jobs and can handle the drinking needs of an average person for a year.

- **Power and lighting**: You should have a lot of the same items that were listed in the section above. Hand crank flashlights, chem lights, headlamps, and extra batteries will come in handy. You should also carry your power bank for any devices because you will never know when you'll find some type of signal.

- **Sleeping supplies**: One person should be designated as the person to carry a tent that can fit everyone who is with you. After that, you should have sleeping bags or space blankets to keep people from sleeping on the ground. Space blankets also make a great expedient shelter to protect yourself from the elements.

- **Ready-to-eat food**: You want foods with a long shelf life, and since this is an emergency, you want things that don't take effort to prepare. This food should be as rich in calories and nutrients as you can find. This is an ideal situation for MREs and canned goods—as long as you remember to pack utensils.

- **Hygienic products**: You should have a toothbrush and toothpaste and toilet paper with you. You can pack soap, but for nuclear survival, invest in shower wipes. Never forget deodorant, either.

- **Important documents**: One person in the family should carry photocopies of essential paperwork. This will help when trying to rebuild society.

- **Fire starting tools**: You should have waterproof matches or a flint stick in your bug out bag. One of the best things you can do, though, is learn how to start a fire primitively.

- **Change of clothing**: It should be seasonally appropriate, but pants and long sleeve shirts are the best clothes to have. You should also include a weatherproof jacket or windbreaker along with your breathing mask.

- **Tools for survival**: This is going to be everything else that fills out your bag. These can include a sewing kit, a cutting tool, a multi-tool, and a paracord.

Maintenance and Replenishment

Regular maintenance is important for your shelter. You want to make sure that you still have plenty of goods to last you and your family, and you want to ensure that none of your stockpiled items are damaged. This is also a great time to rotate things out, so set out one day every four months (at minimum) for this task.

The first thing you will do is check on your supplies. You want to make sure there are no pest infestations or damages to the shelter that could affect your supplies. Bagged items should be free of holes and tears. Canned goods should be free from rust, dents, or swelling. This is a great time to check things like batteries to make sure there is no corrosion. Power banks should be fully charged and generators should be maintained if applicable. Even if all your supplies are in pristine condition, you should still do a shelter inspection and address any issues that may arise. If everything looks to be in good condition, you can start the rotation and replenishment process.

Let's start with the gear and clothing in the shelter. When you are moving into the colder months, you want to have warmer changes of clothes, warm gloves, snow boots, and anything else appropriate for the season. You'll do the same thing in the warmer months. This will help you tremendously if you must be conservative with space, but it also lets you make sure that these items still fit properly.

The next items to rotate are personal medications and any other first aid items. Remember the "first in, first out" rule—the oldest medicines need to come out either for use or to be discarded, and new medications should take their place. This won't be difficult with prescriptions, but you should always be mindful of dates. After that, you will do the same with your food items. The initial list you made of how much you and your family would need should still be on hand, and you always want to maintain that number.

Evacuation Plans and Staying Informed

Family Emergency Plan

Every home should have an emergency plan that addresses a range of disasters from gas leaks to natural disasters. By identifying these emergencies and practicing your plan frequently, you will be ready for whatever may come.

The first thing you need to do is identify all emergency scenarios. This could be a house fire, a gas leak, or something that could happen. Then, you should identify the natural disasters that are unique to where you live. Finally, you will identify the outliers like nuclear war. When you identify them, you will determine if you need to shelter in place or if you need to evacuate.

You have to be prepared for anything, so you need to be prepared for a time when your family is separated. You should have two meeting places for your family—one near your home and one outside of the neighborhood. After you determine these meeting places, you need to figure out a primary route and a backup route to reach these locations. If you are separated and your meeting locations or routes to get to them are no longer functional, you should have an emergency contact who isn't in the area. Everyone should have this contact's cell phone number and a landline number for them. This allows everyone to call and check in, and it gives you a chance to send them all instructions on where to meet.

Evacuating the Area

The closer you are to a point of impact, the more likely it will be that you need to evacuate. There is going to be a lot of panic with multiple people who all have the same idea as you, but there are some things you can do to avoid any delays.

The first thing is knowing your routes. No matter where you are, you should be able to evacuate at a moment's notice. Whether it be from home, school, work, or anywhere—knowing all potential routes is important. You also want to make sure that everyone in your household knows the evacuation destination. Again, this is if you become separated with no way to contact each other.

One of the biggest considerations you are going to have is transportation. You want a reliable bug out vehicle (BOV); otherwise, you and your family are going to be in for a long hike through a devastated land. With nuclear warfare, all electronics are going to be affected by EMPs, which are going to disable all modern cars. Therefore, if you are going to buy a BOV, you want something much older without all the computer chips and other advances. Your BOV should always be ready to go; meaning that everything is in great running condition and that it has a full tank of gas or diesel.

Communication Options in Nuclear Survival or Grid Down Scenario

The first communications are ones we are a bit more familiar with, and they are great to have when conventional phone lines are tied up or knocked offline. I will preface this by saying that these are methods that are at the mercy of electromagnetic pulses released during a nuclear strike. If there is a large-scale nuclear war, there is a significant possibility that these means of communication will all be lost.

- **Emergency weather radio**: Above anything, a weather radio is a great way to stay up-to-date on local and national situations like weather reports and other vital information. These radios are a must-have because they can operate without electricity as long as you have batteries. You can also find solar-powered models and hand-crank radios.

- **Two-way radios**: These radios work on a designated frequency, and they are great for communicating over short distances. If you plan on scouting the area after an attack, this is a great way to stay in contact with those still in the shelter.

- **Ham radio**: These radios are a more sophisticated radio-communications system that requires you to have a license before you can operate them. Ham radios can span long distances, which makes them useful for trying to reach out to emergency responders and communities that are acting as safe havens.

- **Satellite phones**: Through a network of satellites, these phones are perfect for areas that have difficulty achieving a signal.

Again, those methods might be lost, which will leave you looking for other ways to signal for help or try to find other survivors. These methods will take some practice, but they are skills that are always going to be useful to you.

- **Message drops**: In instances where communication lines are down, you can still leave messages for other people by using these message drops. This will take coordination with the people you are trying to communicate with if you want to leave specific messages. You can also leave messages in what look to be high-traffic areas for others to find.

- **Messenger pigeons**: It may sound far-fetched, but if you have access to messenger pigeons, then you should put them to use. Pigeons have been used for centuries to send messages, and they are often trained to fly to and from specific locations.

- **Morse code**: This is a communication system that uses dots and dashes to represent numbers and letters, but what makes this versatile is that you can use a flashlight, whistle, or anything else to send messages out.

- **Smoke signals**: Smoke signals are another method of communication that has been used for centuries. When you build a fire, there will be a column of smoke that you can manipulate into patterns by using a blanket or something else to interrupt the smoke. Basic starting and stopping of the smoke will let others know where you are, and if you are skilled enough, you can send Morse code messages this way, too.

- **Hand signals**: It's going to be a wild world out there, and there may be times when you are forced to move silently to avoid drawing attention. Hand signals can convey simple messages over short distances.

When you are preparing for a nuclear war, the primary goal is to put as much distance between you and any fallout as possible. The farther away you are, the better. After distance, your next best option is shielding yourself. It's important to remember that the fallout dust and other particles will lose their potency fairly quickly. That doesn't mean it's completely safe; it just means that you can carefully leave your shelter and get to a safer location or find other survivors. As long as you wear a mask to avoid breathing in the dust and wear protective clothing, you will be okay.

Aside from stockpiling your supplies and trying to keep everyone in that shelter calm, your biggest issue is going to be finding filters and air pumps that are independent of the power grid. These hand-cranked filters can be found, but you want to make sure that you are getting positive pressure. This is how you can keep only fresh air coming in and not fallout particles.

Before we move on, there might be some of you who are in a position that might seem scary. Survival chances drop the closer you are to potential targets. This is where underground shelters are going to be an absolute must. They also need to be airtight and equipped with firefighting equipment to give yourself a better chance at surviving.

Chapter 3:

Signs the Apocalypse May Be Near

All war is absurd. For thousands of years, human beings have chosen to settle their differences by obliterating one another. And when we are not obliterating one another, we spend an enormous amount of time and attention coming up with better ways to obliterate one another and the next time around. It's all a little strange, if you think about it. –Malcom Gladwell, The Bomber Mafia: A Dream, a Temptation, and the Longest Night of the Second World War

Prepping for nuclear war looks the same as prepping for any major disaster, but now we need to turn our focus solely on nuclear weapons and an impending apocalypse. How will we know the warning signs? What are the major targets? How do we know if the war has already begun, and what are the signs of nuclear winter? Knowing these things and keeping a watchful eye on the world around you will increase your odds of survival.

Is World War III on the Horizon?

This is every prepper's first question when trying to gear up for a nuclear war. Since the end of WWII, people across the world have been guessing or trying to predict when the next world war would start. It has happened so much now that "World War III" seems to be a constant buzzword on the news or a trending topic on the internet, and as such, people often just brush it off. It's a "boy who cried wolf" situation; when you hear something so much and it doesn't happen, it's easy to not believe in it. However, the threat is very real, so you should take it upon yourself to look for signs of an imminent nuclear war.

Openly Talking About New Weapon Technology

It shouldn't be a surprise that the nuclear nations are making new advancements in weapons technology. It's also no surprise that nations that can't build their own weapons are trying to procure them in legal ways or on the black market. The commonality throughout the world, though, is that these nations typically handle their business quietly. So, why would a country announce plans or unveil its military advancements, and is it a sign of an impending nuclear war?

Nations will usually talk about these things when they want to put the rest of the world in a defensive position. It's typically an idle threat made to give a nation the upper hand. It can also be a sign of an impending war, but that's largely dependent on the response to the announcement.

Frequency and Location of Missile Tests

Weapon testing happens frequently in every nation. They need to make sure that the missiles they have—as well as new designs—work properly. Tests are also run to test military response to those weapons. But there are times when these tests become more of a threat.

The first sign is frequent tests. A country wouldn't need to do multiple tests with a weapon unless they are planning to use it. The next sign is testing weapons close to an opposing country's border. There are occurrences of this already with the missile tests done by North Korea. While they pass it off as a routine "weapons test," it is usually taken as a serious threat.

Global Political Turmoil

The first part of this is the trickiest part to read as a sign, and that is political rhetoric. World leaders can make direct or passive threats, which we have seen happen with North Korea in the 2010s and most recently with Russia when the Ukraine war started. What makes rhetoric hard to read is that they could be making idle threats to see how other countries would respond.

However, a sign that something major is happening will be when a country withdraws its ambassador, or they cut off any diplomacy with other countries. Even during extremely tense periods, the lines of communication between countries remain open. So, if everything breaks down and a country refuses to reach a solution, war is sure to come.

Government Officials Bugging Out

If there is an imminent threat to the nation or, say, the president's life, the secret service will move them to an undisclosed location to protect their life. Something like this won't be public knowledge, but you might notice news outlets commenting about not knowing where the president is. While this can be a strong indicator of something like a nuclear war, you should start looking to other government officials to give you a much clearer sign.

If the president's cabinet, members of Congress, and the vice-president are evacuated or moved to undisclosed locations, this is a much better sign of impending disaster. Their lives matter for the rebuilding of the nation, so these parties will always be the first to get to safety.

Military Branches Going on Alert

Seeing an increase in military activity might be a good sign that things are taking a turn for the worst. Most of our nuclear armament is controlled by the Air Force, with the rest being handled by the Navy. If you notice more fighter jets or bomber jets in the skies running drills or lingering near potential targets, this can be a better sign.

But as strong as these signs are, it's virtually impossible to know when bases go on alert or what the threat level is like. While it could help to know someone on active duty or a news correspondent stationed on the base, most of these people are held to the same standard as the rest of the military. Therefore, confirmation won't be given to you until the military is ready.

Word From News Outlets, Agencies, or the Internet

You'd hope that you would get some kind of confirmation of World War 3 or a nuclear attack, but, again, news outlets are not going to announce anything until they are given the "okay" from the government. This is largely because the panic would be too great. Instead of calmly seeking shelter, it will be chaos. What about government agencies? They are also trying to avoid the devastation of mass panic, and they are concerned with getting top government officials and other notable people into shelters. You'll get confirmation of war from these places, but it will likely be a delayed confirmation.

The last place to turn is the internet. While it has been a useful tool to spread information, it takes a long time to sift through it all. Now that anyone can buy verification for their accounts, it adds difficulty in sorting through misinformation.

Again, relying on one source or one sign is not a great idea. Instead, look for combinations of these signs before deciding your next move.

Most Likely Targets

Not knowing if you are going to get confirmation of nuclear war in a timely manner should be enough for you to look at where you live. You could be in an area that is deemed a target by enemy nations and our own government agencies.

ICBM Bases

While there are other military bases that are going to be targets, the ones in the most danger are the ones that can launch a counterattack. One of the greatest threats with ICBM bases is that they are most likely to be attacked with ground detonation nuclear weapons while holding their own deployed nuclear weapons. There are three in the country, and if they were attacked, that could spell disaster for a wide radius around these bases.

The first is Francis E. Warren AFB near Cheyenne, Wyoming. This is the home to the 90th Missile Wing, and while it is a military base, it is still very close to a densely populated area, which we will come back to shortly. Next is Malmstrom AFB, which is outside of Great Falls, Montana. It is home to the 341st Missile Wing, and much like Warren AFB, it is close to a densely populated city.

The third ICBM base is at Minot AFB, which is in Minot, North Dakota. Because the area isn't heavily populated, casualties will be much lower from the initial impact. But as one nuclear weapon triggers others, an attack on this base could spread radioactive fallout hundreds of miles away.

Other Military Bases

Just because bases don't have ICBMs doesn't mean that they will be safe during the initial attacks. For example, Hill AFB in Utah would be a target because this base acts as a nuclear storage depot. The same applies to Kirtland AFB in Albuquerque, New Mexico, which is near the Los Alamos Laboratory.

Another target will be the bases that have the submarines and planes that will act as the second response to a nuclear attack after ICBMs. There is the Naval Submarine Base Kings Bay in Georgia and Naval Base Kitsap in Washington state which are major submarine hubs. Whiteman AFB and Barksdale AFB house planes that can fly at subsonic speeds and carry nuclear payloads. There is no doubt that these will be under attack with ground-burst nuclear weapons.

Other military bases will be targeted because they act as major command and control centers for the military. The Pentagon will likely be a first-wave target because it is one of the most important centers for our military. Strategic Command at Offutt AFB will be another target, and so will NORAD in Colorado. Without these bases online, it will be almost impossible to organize a response to an attack.

The same applies to the low-frequency stations that are in place to communicate with submarines. There's the VLF Transmitter Cutler in Maine, the VLF Transmitter Lualualei in Hawaii, and the Jim Creek Naval Radio Station in Washington state.

This doesn't even account for the bases that are in densely populated areas or the ones that are being turned into hubs for nuclear weapons like Dyess AFB in Texas.

Densely Populated Areas and Landmarks

Cities with large, dense populations are going to be first or second-wave targets in a large-scale attack. Places like Washington D.C., San Francisco, Los Angeles, Houston, Chicago, and New York could be some of the first to fall in an attack followed by other densely populated areas. So, what does an attacking nation stand to gain, and just how bad will these attacks be?

The attacks themselves are going to be devastating. When a city is densely populated, evacuation becomes virtually impossible. Even if one does make it out of the city, all the major roads leading out are gridlocked. This is going to contribute to most of the casualties in a nuclear war, and it's going to bring the chances of rebuilding to almost zero.

Another reason attacking nations are going to target large cities is that many of them are home to crucial pieces of our infrastructure. Major financial and technological institutions, energy plants, major (non-military) government agencies, and wireless transmission systems are all housed in these cities. Again, this will affect how quickly—and if—we are able to rebuild after the war.

After the major metropolitan areas, the next targets are going to be other important cities like state capitals. Eliminating as much of the government as we know it will make post-war life extremely difficult, and it will make any chance of retaliation impossible. Another late-wave attack would likely see the nuclear power plants around the country destroyed, which will release 11 more radioactive materials into the air. Landmarks like the Hoover Dam and other things that represent our country might be destroyed in much later attacks, but if these places are destroyed, it will no doubt be done to take away any morale that may be left.

What to Do During the Blast

Taking what you learned about a nuclear blast and its effects, combined with knowing how close you are to potential targets, will determine your survival odds and what you need to do to increase those odds.

Your first consideration is going to be the distance between you and the bomb. The epicenter of a nuclear explosion is going to be the most lethal. Even those who seek shelter underground won't be able to breathe as all the air is going to be pulled away to fuel the fireball. The next layer is the blast radius. Survival becomes possible, but there is a higher chance of thermal burns and radiation exposure, not to mention the overpressurization that will level most structures. As you get more distance from the target, the better your survival chances become.

While you will have higher odds, you will do best to remember that there is no guaranteed safe option in a nuclear war. It's all going to depend on how many bombs are dropped, the power of those bombs, and if it was an air or surface explosion. Even wind patterns can affect you, to boot.

If there is ample warning of a nuclear attack and you are not in the immediate blast radius, your best bet is to get to shelter, even when you are away from your personal shelter. Seek out underground shelters first, but if none are available, concrete or steel structures will be sufficient. If you are in the blast radius, your only option is an underground shelter, but you want to ensure that there are multiple exit points. As other buildings are knocked down, they could begin covering up that shelter's exits.

But what happens if there is no shelter around? This is a lot like sheltering from a tornado; you want to be in the central part of the structure. This means you should be away from windows, and you should be covering yourself with as many materials as you can to protect yourself from any debris that might be hurled through the air. If there is plenty of warning ahead of the blast, you can work on boarding up windows like those in hurricane areas do. After that, make sure gas lines and other utilities are shut off. At the very least, you want to ensure that your heating or AC units are off to prevent the structure from being filled with fallout. You can also work on sealing doors and vents if there is time. This can be done with plastic sheeting and duct tape, but even after this, you should still move to the center of the structure and cover yourself. Cut down any chance of exposure by covering your mouth and nose.

After you are confident that the attacks have stopped, then you need to get out of the area. You are going to be looking for medical attention and somewhere far from the blasts. Even if you weren't affected by the blasts, you are now dealing with radioactive fallout that is still likely "hot," so follow all your decontamination procedures when it's safe to do so.

Coping With Fallout and Nuclear Winter

Fallout

I will cover this more in detail in the next chapter, but emerging from your shelter and seeing the world coated in nuclear fallout is going to be an apocalyptic sign. The radioactivity of this dust is going to greatly depend on your location from the blast. Those places farther away will need to exercise caution, albeit not as much caution as those closer to the blasts will need to have.

There will be no way to completely avoid fallout after the bombs have dropped, but it shouldn't be something to fear. With extra caution, you will be able to navigate a post-nuclear war world.

There is no better time than now to go and get radiation measuring equipment. This will keep you away from radioactive hotspots, and it will make sure that you aren't bringing radioactive particles into your shelter. This also means you should be fitting your shelter with the proper ventilation and filtration systems. By finding systems that provide clean air while keeping harmful particles out, you are further ensuring that all the shelter inhabitants are safe. It also won't hurt to stockpile filters for these systems, too, since they don't have a "use by" date.

Leaving your shelter is going to be a must unless you have a fortress, which means you will need to decontaminate people, pets, items, or anything else coming in from the outside world. Fortunately, fallout won't "soak" through things, which means a simple dusting off or changing out of your protective clothes will be sufficient. The only time you need to worry about the dust is if the radioactive elements of it are still extremely high, which can be determined by your measuring and monitoring equipment.

The last consideration with nuclear fallout is going to be food and water safety. Hunting and taking water from open sources is going to be almost impossible unless you are absolutely positive that there is no radiation present. So, what about scavenging for food and water? This is very possible as long as you're exercising caution and being mindful of radioactive areas. Typically, any food and water that you find will be safe as long as the seals haven't been broken.

Nuclear fallout is going to be scary to see, but it will be easy to navigate these areas safely. But now, we have to discuss a sign of the apocalypse that we can't just "navigate around."

Nuclear Winter

Immediately after the bombs fell over Nagasaki and Hiroshima, scientists began studying what the effects of nuclear warfare could be. They already knew that large-scale explosions would have an adverse effect on the environment. One of their greatest examples came in 1815 after the eruption of Mount Tambora, which was the largest volcanic eruption known to humanity. The eruption sent massive amounts of smoke, ash, and other particles into the air. These particles would travel across the planet, putting a screen between us and the sun. What followed was catastrophic. The planet cooled, crops failed, and famine soon set in. It was known as the "year without a summer."

As long as nuclear weapons have been used, research has been done to study what would follow small-scale and large-scale nuclear wars. This is how we have the doomsday scenario of nuclear winter—a global event that would be lethal to billions of people who survived the initial strikes.

We can start with a small-scale war, which is something that could happen between countries like Pakistan and India. This type of war could have the same effects that Mount Tambora had. The planet would become chilled enough that there would be one year of massive crop failures across the globe. It's survivable with the right stockpile, but what happens if the scale of the war increases?

A large-scale nuclear war between Russia and the United States would be devastating to the environment. The amount of smoke, dust, and ash that would be launched into the atmosphere would be so great that instead of a screen between us and the sun, it would be a thick barrier.

Planet temperatures would plummet and become colder than the last ice age, and this effect could span decades. Without a sufficient amount of sunlight and warmth, a lot of plant life will be wiped out. Animals will be next, followed by humans. The famine would be so great that alone, it could be lethal to over 5 billion people.

When you know what to expect, it helps you to make timely and rational decisions. With nuclear war, there is a lot to expect that we aren't quite sure of yet. There are things now that can help you even further. For instance, the next time you are out, find the area that would be used as shelter in whatever structure you're in. Look for escape routes out of that structure and routes to get away that aren't on the main roadways.

Now, start looking for all these things everywhere—work, public spaces, school. After enough practice, you will be able to go anywhere and immediately spot the safest areas and escape routes.

Chapter 4:

Surviving After World War III

We still live with this unbelievable threat over our heads of nuclear war. I mean, are we stupid? Do we think that the nuclear threat has gone, the destruction of the planet is not imminent? It's a delusion to think it's gone away. –Kevin Costner

Surviving the initial blasts will be a feat in itself, but that is the start of what will be the most difficult period in human history. There is that time right after the bombs stop and before the world starts rebuilding where the only thing that matters is survival. This chapter will give insight into that tumultuous time. What's the first thing you should do after the blast? How do you protect yourself from radiation and other survivors who have ill intentions? What do you do in a world without doctors? Do you stay put, or is it time to bug out? There are so many questions, and the solutions are all in things that preppers practice regularly.

What to Do After the Blast

While Sheltering

You should brace yourself for a while after a nuclear attack to make sure that the aftereffects have stopped. You want to make sure that there are no tremors triggered by the bombs or structures still falling. After major disasters, you will have an idea of when this is because of the quiet that seems to follow.

Now that you and the other people in your shelter can stop bracing, it's time to make the initial assessment. This is just asking out loud if everyone is okay. If someone is in distress or injured, they can speak up for immediate attention. If everyone is okay, use a few moments to collect your thoughts and process what just happened. Once you're feeling better and can think clearer, you can go check on everyone individually; handling any injuries they may have suffered.

After you assess physical injuries, you should assess the mental well-being of everyone in the shelter. This is going to be a traumatic event, so you want to make sure that everyone gets to a place of rational thinking before moving on. This is going to take comfort or a distraction, but the time spent addressing this will make things later run much smoother.

If you are in your shelter, you likely have enough of everything you are going to need. However, you should still be making a quick assessment of what you have. This is to make sure you have enough supplies (medical, food, water) and that nothing has been damaged. You also want to test out your flashlights and see if there are any operational radio stations.

Needless to say, things will be drastically different if you have to take an expedient shelter. This may put you in a shelter with people you are unfamiliar with, but you still need to be a leader with the knowledge you have. If there are other people in this area, you should make sure they are okay and aren't in need of immediate care. If the initial check goes well, you should assess all supplies first. Is there a first aid kit there? Do you have food and water? Are there any tools that can act as protection? Are there extra clothes or anything that you can use as an expedient mask? Doing this assessment will allow you to make a calm, thought-out plan about what you need to do next. You can follow this up with the individual assessments of the individuals there.

When You Are Planning to Leave

The last section of this chapter is about how to make the best decision for sheltering or bugging out, but if you plan to leave, you now need to think about some other survival needs like protection.

You can't rule out the possibility that there will be some bad people out there, even after a nuclear war. There could even be survivors who are willing to do anything to get much-needed supplies or shelter. In either case, you are going to have to stand up to those individuals to protect yourself and others around you. What supplies should you be thinking of for self-defense? Should you have multiple? What are their pros and cons? Do you really have to have things like this?

First of all, you are better served by having weapons around for protection. One aspect of apocalyptic depictions from movies and TV shows—lawlessness—is certainly going to be a reality. There will be no more police and no more courts left to uphold justice, which will lead to a newfound danger. Having protection is going to prevent you from becoming a victim. Now that we have that settled, let's get into all the weapons you can potentially have.

Impact Weapons

Impact weapons, or trauma weapons, are the most primitive forms of self-defense weapons we have. They are objects you can hold at one end while hitting an attacker with the other end. Bats, clubs, sledgehammers, maces, and batons make for reliable impact weapons. There are also others like whips, chains, or nunchucks that add flexibility to the weapon.

These weapons can be purposefully made or you can have a DIY weapon like a two-by-four or a lead pipe, so a pro to these is that they can be anything you find. They can also be modified for more severe damage—think of a board with nails stuck in it. Another pro is that you can keep an attacker out of reach, and these weapons are also great if you are looking for non-lethal protection or simply want to disarm an attacker.

One of the biggest drawbacks to impact weapons is that the attacker has to be in range in order to use it. This could turn bad if they are equipped with a firearm. You also have to be strategic with your hits. Every second matters, which means you become vulnerable each time you draw the weapon back.

Projectile Weapons

These weapons are anything that you can throw at an attacker to inflict damage, given that you know how to use them. These could be boomerangs, spears, or javelins. Bows and arrows, crossbows, throwing axes, or throwing knives are also great examples of projectile weapons.

When you are under attack, you ideally want to avoid close-quarters combat. Keeping the attacker out of reach cuts down on the chances of them striking and injuring you, especially if you are at a significant disadvantage in size. Projectile weapons are a great way to keep an attacker away while being more efficient than impact weapons. Though, the right type of spear or javelin can act as a projectile and impact weapon.

The biggest drawback to these weapons is going to be your skill level. You have to have a good aim, and you have to have enough power behind your throws for the weapon to be effective. Another disadvantage is knowing that these weapons are likely to be lost if you aren't taking lethal action.

Bladed Weapons

The first bladed weapons were used during the Bronze Age (around 1700 BC), and they were capable of causing severe wounds with one movement. You will have several options here, especially because you can use the cutting tool in your bug out bag. Knives, daggers, shivs, and some smaller axes are portable and relatively lightweight. You can also use full-size axes or swords if you still want to keep your distance from attackers.

One of the best reasons to have a bladed weapon is how quickly they can end an attack. This will keep you from having to tap into your stamina, especially if there are multiple attackers. You also can't forget that these weapons can also double as kitchenware to cut up dinner.

Bladed weapons aren't as efficient as they sound, though. While a cut could slow an attacker down, they are likely not going to feel it during an adrenaline high. It would take a strategic move to land a debilitating blow. Smaller bladed weapons are going to force you into close-quarters combat. Weapons like swords and full-size axes are going to be more of a drawback because you have to have prior experience with these weapons.

Firearms

Firearms changed battles forever, and they will still be defining weapons to use in a post-apocalyptic world. You can opt for smaller pistols for portability, a semi-automatic rifle for a more powerful but portable option, or you can get a rifle with a scope for long-distance strikes.

There are several advantages to these weapons. In most cases, one shot is going to be debilitating to an attacker. There's a pretty high potential that an attacker will flee at the sight of a firearm. And, of course, a firearm can be useful when hunting, if you find hunting grounds that are safe from radiation.

But these weapons have some very large disadvantages. Firearms are loud, and when the world is quiet after nuclear war, you will be heard from miles away. This makes you an attractive target with scavengers or other groups needing protection. Also, any surviving ammunition is going to be scarce, and when you run out of ammo, your firearms will become obsolete.

Protecting Yourself From Radiation Poisoning

After the wars have fallen silent, non-impact areas are going to be suffering from extreme amounts of radiation. Any amount of time out in a "wasteland" is going to expose you to harmful amounts of radiation, which will lead to radiation poisoning. The severity of this poisoning is going to come from the amount of radiation that was absorbed by your body, which is called "the dose." The other factors will be the type of radiation, how you came into contact with it, and the length of time of exposure.

A small amount of radiation can be harmful, but the effects will not show up in your body for years, decades, or not at all. However, you might have been exposed to a large amount of harmful radiation in a short period of time, which can lead to acute radiation syndrome (ARS). The symptoms can set in within minutes, or they can be delayed by a few days, but the following are the symptoms you should look for:

- skin burns

- nausea

- vomiting

To avoid this from happening, you need to remember these three things: distance, shielding, and time.

- **Distance**: This is simple; get as much distance between yourself and the area where fallout particles are falling.

- **Shielding**: If you are trapped in a suburban area, or if you have a shelter at the ready, then running off might not be the best option for you. This is why materials matter: Heavier and denser materials like concrete and brick are going to act as a shield from those particles and the radiation they carry.

- **Time**: The longer you can wait, the better off you will be. At the very least, you want to wait 24 hours (12 in an absolute emergency). Fallout is going to lose its radioactive potency rapidly, and you should be at your most cautious for the first two weeks. By then, it will only be around one percent of its initial radiation.

If you are caught outside or in an expedient shelter without supplies during the peak of radioactivity, you will need to move to a safer location. This needs to be done quickly and calmly, and as long as you take the following precautions, you will stay safe out there. As you are getting to a safe place, brush off the clothes you are wearing every few minutes. Keep as much radioactive fallout off of you as possible.

As soon as you make it to that safer place, your first goal is to get the exposed clothing into sealable bags. If there isn't a sealable bag available, then just find something to put the clothing in to set it outside of the shelter. After that, you will need to rinse off the rest of the fallout, especially any that might be lingering in your hair. Yes, this will use up some of your water reserves, but it must be done. It's also one of those factors you should consider when stockpiling supplies. If you can get something like a camping shower into your shelter, this will be extremely helpful. You can take a shower with soap and shampoo to make sure you get all the fallout particles off.

Once you are clean and in clean clothes, the next few days will be spent monitoring your symptoms. Keep taking your potassium iodide tablets, and if you don't feel anything after those few days, you should be ready to make your next plan.

Navigating Through a Contaminated Environment

No matter how long it has been since the bombs dropped, your first exploration of your area or any new locations is going to be an event that you should be cautious about. This is why it's a good idea to have some sort of radiation meter on hand. This will keep you safe by helping you avoid radioactive hot spots.

There are several types of meters available, which can make it hard to figure out which one is the "right one" for you. While I will go over the types of these readers, remember that nothing will replace hands-on experience to learn how to read a meter and what it's detecting. This makes it important to shop for meters from reputable dealers who can tell you more about what you are going to buy.

- **Handheld survey meters**: When you think of radiation meters, you likely think of a Geiger counter. Most handheld survey meters are used to detect contamination at a surface level and on people, which is why they are typically what is used at radiological or nuclear facilities to maintain federal compliance. These are limited, though, because they require training to read the meter properly. There are also several types that use different methods of detection or unit scale, which can make detecting while navigating a difficult task.

- **Personal dosimeter**: These are small monitors that can be worn like a ring, and they measure accumulated radiation doses. Because of how they read radiation and where they are worn, you will get a very accurate reading. But therein lies the problem: As the reading is done passively, you will not get a real-time reading. Personal dosimeters are great to have just to monitor radiation levels you take on each time you're out of your shelter, but they will not help you navigate.

- **Pocket ionization chamber**: These meters are around the size of a pen, which makes them portable. You just look through the meter to see the deflection of the needle that's inside. Different models will let you get readings of various exposure ranges, and these meters are great because they don't need batteries to operate. They operate in real-time, and you really don't need to do much work except "charging" them before use. However, it is limited in use because you do have to stop and look into the meter, which can mean precious seconds spent in highly radioactive areas. It is also hindered by only being able to read within specific dose ranges, and you could also get false readings if the device is mechanically shocked.

- **Electronic personal dosimeter**: These meters can read high ranges of exposure, and they have an alarm that will sound when you are at the threshold of a preset amount of exposure. These dosimeters are used by radiation workers in planned exposure situations because they can help control exposure and also be used as a survey meter. While they are used for places with potential radiation exposure, they aren't as useful in emergency situations. Much of this hindrance is because of the preset parameters, but it also comes from these devices not having large displays and loud alarms.

- **Personal emergency radiation detectors (PERDs)**: These detectors are worn on the body, and they have presets for exposure rate or accumulated dosage. They are the detectors that most first responders will use because of their ability to read high exposure rates, which makes them useful in cold, hot, and dangerous zones. A small problem—and really the only issue with these monitors—is that they do need a steady dose rate, which can affect their use in a cold zone.

  o There are also non-alarming PERDs, which are the size of a credit card and give you a visual sign of the exposure levels of an area. As exposure increases, the sensitive area will start getting darker. These PERDs are great backups, and they are perfect if you are in a situation where you need to be silent. The only real drawback to these monitors is that it can be hard to understand the readings, and much like the powered version, they won't read exposures under a certain level.

- **Extended range personal radiation detectors (ER-PRDs)**: Detectors like this have a dual detector system, which means you can read low and high dose ranges. They will track the real-time exposure rate and the accumulated exposure rates, which is helpful for navigating new areas that might have been close to impact sites. The only drawback with ER-PRDs comes with their alarm settings. You have to set the range to match your needs, but this has to be done with each new task. Having those alarms means that you are going to have a low-end setting, which can become a problem when you're in high-exposure areas.

When you are getting ready to make your first trips out of the shelter, it is important to remember that these first trips are for surveying the area. Are there any radioactive hot spots? Is there any damage at all in your area? Having a radiation detector will make sure you stay safe during these trips.

So, what should you be looking for? You should always be keeping your eye out for escape routes, which means ensuring there are no major roadblocks or other damage. This will help you establish safe travel paths in case you have to bug out.

This could be a good time to search and scavenge for any supplies, which is where your protection weapons will be helpful. But one of the most important things you will be looking for when you're out there is survivors.

Life Without Doctors

While we can never say for sure what the world is going to look like after a nuclear war, it is better to just assume that the first responders we are accustomed to will be nonexistent. Police, EMTs, firefighters, and most certainly medical professionals are all going to be devastated by the war, and those who survive the attacks are going to either set up centralized bases or deploy themselves to the more affected regions. In short, you are now going to be in charge of any injuries that occur.

Naturally, this is going to be where your medical stockpile and first aid kits are going to come into play. But do you know how to use those supplies? Stockpiles are worthless if you don't have the knowledge to use them.

It's important to act now and get the proper training that can save your life or someone else's. Find out if there are any CPR and first aid courses in your area. These courses will teach you how to handle an array of emergencies like shock, broken bones, burns, cuts, and other injuries that could be common in a post-nuclear world. What's even more helpful is getting some hands-on practice. Knowing how to handle these severe emergencies will help you keep calm when dealing with them in real-time. If there are no classes being offered in your community, talk to the local first responders about getting some classes arranged.

Of course, you are taking these classes to help yourself and your family, but that also means helping anyone who is injured. Not only is it the right thing to do, but having some medical knowledge is a great bartering tool in a disaster situation. The stranger you help might have access to food or supplies. They could even have a much more sophisticated shelter with a large stockpile of goods. Bartering and helping strangers is going to be the first step you can take in rebuilding the world.

Besides taking courses, find as many resources as you can that you can call upon in emergency situations. Some great books that you can add to your survival collection are David Werner's *When There Is No Doctor*, Murray Dickson's *When There Is No Dentist*, and *The Survival Medicine Handbook* by Joseph and Amy Alton.

Bugging In or Bugging Out

One of the toughest decisions you're going to make is knowing when to stay put and when to bug out. That won't change after a nuclear war. Even if you have the means to stay and your shelter is secured, you should always be ready to bug out at a moment's notice. So, when should you think about leaving, and is there a safe way to do so?

Some examples of when bugging out after nuclear war would be necessary are:

- running low on supplies in the shelter

- natural disasters in the area. These become more dangerous as all structures could be compromised after the war.

- dangerous people settling in the area. Just because they are rebuilding some things, they might not have the best of intentions with people that weren't in the group.

- severe medical emergencies. Although you should have knowledge of a lot of things regarding first aid, there could always be a situation that you alone cannot handle.

- being the only survivor. If it's just you and your family, you owe it to them and the reconstruction of humanity to bug out so you can find other survivors.

With that being said, this is a different world, and it is going to be dangerous any way you view it. There are going to be radioactive areas to avoid and contaminated supplies to sift through. You're also going to want to explore unfamiliar territories. While you may live in the area, how well-versed are you in its layout? Another uncertainty will come from the people around you. It's a lawless world, and there could be people out there who do not mean well. So, how can you bug out effectively, while staying safe?

- Above everything else, you need to stay calm. Do not panic or make rash decisions. Bugging out after a nuclear war is going to take full concentration.

- Take your radiation meter. This will save you a lot of time when it comes to finding supplies out in the wild. You will also avoid those radioactive hot spots as you're making your way out of the area.

- Take your protection weapons. The sight of a weapon alone could deter a potential attacker. Your main goal should be to avoid sketchy people. If they attack, then you want to disarm them. Anything beyond avoidance and disarmament will come because there is a serious threat to your life.

- When it comes to people and places, you want to keep a lookout in all directions. There could be traps in front of you or on the ground, or there could be an ambush from an enemy group. You and your group should move together and strategically—with eyes surveying the area.

- Another pair of tools you should have with you are detailed maps and a compass. Having these tools and knowing how to use them will make your bugging out trip much easier, as you can avoid large cities and any other potential hotspots.

Chapter 5:

Rebuilding After the Bomb Drops

In nuclear war all men are cremated equal. –Dexter Gordon

The Harsh Reality of Nuclear War

One of the hardest aspects of preparing for doomsday scenarios is that everything seems relatively easy because you're not in the thick of it. Much like with nuclear war. It's easy to say: "Get to shelter," "Learn how to render aid," "Get back out there and rebuild." However, the world that we are "getting back into" is going to be something we can never imagine. So, while we have gone over what to expect in a nuclear and post-nuclear world, it should be touched on one more time.

Black Rains

A nuclear bomb detonates. The area immediately at the detonation site will be vaporized, followed by a blast wave that will level everything within a specific radius. A massive fireball will rise, and separate fires will begin to catch on everything left standing. Smoke, dust, and fallout are being carried into the atmosphere, which is going to produce weather events that are unique to a nuclear blast. One of those events is black rain.

Black rain is a thick, black blob that falls from the sky. It has the consistency of oil, but if it comes into contact with your skin, you will be exposed to more radiation than if you were to walk into the epicenter of the blast. The radiation is so potent that it will immediately begin to make changes to a person's DNA.

Around 20 minutes after the bomb detonated over Hiroshima, black rain fell over the city. Those who were around didn't know better, and since the heat and lack of oxygen were making them dehydrated, they drank the falling rain. It was a fatal mistake, and the areas where the rains fell still hold some of that radiation. So, when you have a large-scale war, affected areas will be widespread.

Devastating Storms

Two or three years after those black rains, the Earth is going to be enveloped in devastating storms. The debris that gets sent up into the sky will block out the sun, but it will change the weather patterns that we are accustomed to. Clouds will now be able to produce rain much more efficiently, so we could see an almost constant rainfall. It will also make severe weather even more devastating.

This will only get worse as you get closer to the coastlines. The planet as a whole may cool down, but the oceans won't cool as fast, which means they will be fairly warm. It will prove to be a brutal combination as hurricanes and typhoons will become larger, extremely powerful, and will increase in frequency.

EMPs

When a nuclear bomb detonates, it is going to send out an electromagnetic pulse that will shut down the electric grid for an area and fry any piece of electronic equipment in that area. Of course, with a large-scale nuclear war, this will likely happen across the world. So, it would take a lot of bombs for the world to be thrown into darkness, right?

Sadly, there would only need to be one bomb. With the right size and payload, a bomb detonated around 300 miles above the US would be powerful enough to shut our entire electrical grid down. Lights will go out and any electronics that aren't protected in a faraday cage will become obsolete. Cities and towns everywhere will lose water treatment facilities, which means that unless someone has a way to pump well water, you only have your reserve water, scavenged water, or you have access to a hand pump well.

If it is only one bomb used as an EMP, the entire country would be in the dark for at least six months, which leaves us vulnerable throughout that time. However, in a large-scale war, strategic bombs will be launched that will cut any chances of reconnecting to a conventional power grid.

No Sun

This is going to be the precursor to the nuclear winter that will follow. Areas near the epicenters of bombs will have so much energy that they will turn almost everything into a combustible material. Buildings, trees, and even paved roads will catch fire. Targeted oil refineries will be targeted, which means they will also be contributing to the thick black cloud of smoke rising into the sky.

This smoke will be heavy with soot, and it is going to be extremely toxic. A cloud that only stretches upward of nine miles will be enough to be caught in the atmosphere and spread across the world. The more clouds of smoke, the more goes into our atmosphere. Eventually, we will be under a black cloud.

For the first few years after the nuclear war, this will be all we see. In a large-scale war, this could be at least 30 years before we see any glimpse of the blue sky.

Nuclear Winter

Now, we've spent some time talking about what would happen in a nuclear winter. The actual temperature drop will depend on how much debris is launched into the atmosphere and how thick of a barrier it forms. However, you should be planning on a drop of at least 30 degrees Fahrenheit, if not colder.

There will most likely be no change in seasons, either. We will be stuck in a perpetual winter until the smoke and debris start to clear out. While the initial effects are great, growing seasons could still be possible as long as there's the slightest sign of sunlight.

It should be noted that nuclear winter is a doomsday scenario within a doomsday scenario. The effects that we know of could be an (over or under) exaggeration.

Crippled Ozone Layer

A year after the bombs are dropped, a hole will start forming in our ozone layer, which will rapidly deteriorate. Even if less than a fraction of a percent of the world's nuclear arsenal is used, it can destroy around half of the ozone layer.

This is the barrier that protects us from the harmful UV rays of the sun. After the black clouds and debris finally dissipate, we will be left with these devastating light rays. Surviving plants will rapidly die out, and even the crops we manage to grow during the nuclear winter will be affected. They will be small, weak, and have difficulty with reproduction.

Other living things will suffer, too, as the UV rays will have numerous adverse effects. The most prominent effect is not being able to go outside for very long. Skin will burn and skin cancer will quickly develop.

The Human Effects

Those who survive the initial blasts still face tremendous hardship. Nuclear winter won't stop crops completely, but the amount harvested will not be enough to keep everyone fed. Again, the crippled ecosystem will reach humans; famine will set in and billions of lives will be lost. These things will happen around you, too, during the first five years after the bombs drop.

Those near coastlines won't be affected as quickly after the war, but our marine life will be devastated quite quickly. Plankton is one of the largest food sources in the ocean, and with the sun being blacked out, that food will be gone. Then, there will be all the radioactive runoff that will seep into the ocean. The ocean creatures that do survive will be much like the animals on land that survive—none will be safe to eat.

The human loss won't be from famine alone, though. People are going to be in competition for the same resources, which is going to give way to violence. We also can't forget that those radioactive particles are still going to rain down in nuclear fallout.

While prolonged exposure is the worst, any exposure to fallout is deadly. Prolonged exposure will take effect quickly, which will see the rapid spread of cancerous cells. But even if the fallout loses its potency, it can still be enough to cause cancer. Life spans are going to be cut short, and birth defects will be the new normal. There is no real determiner on how long the human race will be plagued by the effects of nuclear weapons. Even today, Scandinavian countries are still having to monitor their farms and animals because of the radiation released at the Chernobyl power plant.

These are all things that we will see in the event of a nuclear war. But while it all looks grim, humans are a resilient life form. One of the first signs of hope that we are going to have is finding or establishing large food supplies. Bottled and canned food is going to be our lifesaver because these things will be the safest food sources after a nuclear war.

If bottles of beer and soda are put near a nuclear blast, they will take on a massive amount of radiation. While the outsides of the bottles will be coated with radiation, the contents will be as safe as they had been before. Bottles that are closest to the detonation site, however, will become radioactive. It won't be enough to be extremely harmful, but the taste profiles will change, so the effects will be noticeable. But taste alone won't matter when we are forced into survival.

Canned food will likely be as safe as bottled drinks. So, any stockpiles are going to become the most valuable items after the war. Those who do have bug out locations are going to have to live in caution, though. Besides their stockpile of food and other supplies, they will probably need to have a hand pump well. As long as the underground supply of water isn't being fed by surface sources, it will still be safe to drink. These lands are going to become sought after and fought over unless an agreement can be made, which will give us a chance to establish the first post apocalyptic communities.

Again, it is hard to see now just how grim a nuclear war and its aftereffects will be. Survivors are going to witness a lot of death, and they are going to be faced with difficult decisions constantly. But, there are those who can adapt to anything and are willing to do whatever it takes to survive. Because of those survivors, the human race will have a chance to rebuild.

Assessing the Damage

Immediately After the Bombs

I touched on this in the last chapter, but now we should dive deeper into the safest procedure for getting out in the world. Remember that if you don't have any reason to be out of your shelter, *do not* leave that shelter. The only reasons you should be out during the immediate aftermath are:

- extreme medical emergencies that you cannot handle

- the bombs have dropped and you're too far from your shelter. If you have supplies and it's feasible to make it back to your home base, then you certainly should be moving there.

- you have limited supplies, so it doesn't make sense to continue to shelter

Other than that, you should be sheltering as long as you possibly can. If you have the means to survive for a long period comfortably, then you should stay there. At most, you can do periodic checks to make sure there are no emergency responders in the area.

You want to avoid as many of the effects of the nuclear bombs and their aftermath as you can. The longer you can ride this out in your shelter, the less potent the radiation will be. After around two weeks, you can do a better check to see if there is or has been anyone else in the area. There might be emergency rescue teams, so it's at least worth it to check. As long as you protect your skin and follow decontamination procedures when you return, this amount of time out of the shelter will be okay.

The First Explorations

Even if you've made peeks at the world or were rushing in the immediate aftermath to your safe area, you are still not fully prepared to see what the landscape looks like now. You will need to take the next steps slowly because it can be extremely easy to get overwhelmed.

Start with an exploration of your immediate neighborhood. Survey the land, the surrounding homes, and the areas you know best. This will let you process and evaluate the impact of the war. You can also use this time to check if there are other people around. Keep in mind, though, that this can quickly become unbearable if you encounter casualties. Again, stick to the areas you know best, and don't stay out for too long.

Return to your shelter and process what you just saw. Allow yourself to deal with any feelings that may have come up, which I will come back to in just a bit.

When you are sure that you are ready to go back out, then your next trip should take you a little further. Maybe go around the entire block or even a few blocks. Find somewhere that you think could be a high-traffic area (clear paths, landmarks, etc.). This is going to be the best place to leave communications for emergency services or potentially other survivors. Remember, you don't want to do this near your shelter as it could attract unwanted attention to you.

By the third trip out, you will have a great idea of the situation, the area, and what the impact was of the nuclear war. Now, you're going to want to identify areas for rebuilding. This type of work should start in the immediate area around your property. You can start there and work outward. If you have found survivors, then you should localize yourselves into a smaller area. After you determine what areas are going to be rebuilt, then you can start making those plans for recovery. Recovery plans are going to involve more surveying trips, but these are going to be focused on other parts of the area's infrastructure.

If you see potential in making the area a recovery effort, then you need to assess the damage to utility lines. While everything is most likely going to be knocked offline in a war, you still need to double-check the utility lines. You are looking for downed power lines, gas leaks, and any breaks in water lines. This is also a great time to find maps of local utility lines if you don't have those in your shelter already. These will tell you where lines run near your property, which will help if there is an underground water source that requires you to dig for a well.

Now you need to check the roads, bridges, and other paths in and out of where you live. There might be an off-chance that you need to bug out of the area. Knowing which paths are still available will help you bug out safely. This also helps you determine how other people can get to where you are, which will help your security measures out when rebuilding. When you are making your assessments, it is important to make detailed notes of everything.

I would also recommend checking those secondary paths around your property, too. Anything that you identify as a route to and away from your home needs to be accounted for after a major disaster.

Dealing With Psychological Trauma

One of the most difficult challenges that we face in a post-nuclear world is dealing with the tremendous amount of psychological trauma that is going to befall those who survive the war. While you can assess and handle the physical medical emergencies with relative ease, there are going to be wounds that go far deeper than what you can see.

To get a better understanding, we need to look at the psychological trauma that is felt after conventional warfare. These are the effects that are felt by those in war-torn countries as well as veterans who try to return to normalcy after being engaged in long-term battles. While everyone is going to feel and exhibit things that are unique to them, there are common factors that determine those long-lasting effects.

- **Intensity of the battle**: While battles happen in waves, they can also be extremely intense during those waves. This can cause a lot of stress on the psyche that typically isn't felt until after the fight-or-flight response has subsided.

- **Group setting**: Being around others during a battle can determine some of the mental effects felt afterward. Even if morale is high, leadership is established, and everyone seems to be working together, much of the negative psychological effects will be present in the aftermath.

- **Battle duration**: Those who live in areas where there is constant fighting and those who are deployed into constant battle zones are going to experience mental fatigue that can lead to psychological trauma. Being involved in fighting that never seems to end can leave a person feeling like there is very little chance of relief coming.

- **Physical hardships**: Living off of limited food and little sleep while forcing the body to operate at these extreme levels can break a person down physically, which can then start affecting their mental state.

- **Living up to expectations**: Whether or not we admit it, we are conditioned to believe that we have to be strong in situations that are difficult. Even in war, people are not only trying to live up to their cultural expectations, but they are also trying to live up to the expectations set on them by their country. When a person is constantly in fear of letting their friends, family, community, and country down, they are putting unnecessary wear on their mental health.

- **Communication**: In the midst of war, it is very likely that lines of communication are severed. On top of the hardships of everything that I listed above, a person is now going to have an added level of anxiety because they don't know the condition of their loved ones.

Again, those are just some of the common effects felt by people in conventional warfare. That didn't even include the anxiety of potentially being taken by enemy forces that people will fear during wartime. Conventional warfare is one thing, but we have no idea what the effects of nuclear warfare are going to be. Our best examples are still Hiroshima and Nagasaki, but we are decades removed from what the world looked like then.

Acute Reactions

Given what we know about war and what we know about mental health now, we can make some better assumptions about what would happen in the aftermath of nuclear war. This first set of symptoms is going to be what would take place within the first few days after the war, but it can even set in minutes or hours after.

- **Motivation**: A catastrophic event like a nuclear war has a numbing effect on a person's mental state. Knowing what is happening outside of your shelter, and understanding that the world you knew is gone, can start to close you off. Instead of getting straight into future survival, you could just "give up." You could also be motivated but in the wrong state of mind. Rather than a panicked response, you could be doing things in a state of deep depression, which can be equally as devastating because you are still losing focus.

- **Dread and panic**: Again, while you may be safe in your shelter, you know what is happening outside. Large-scale destruction and the lingering effects of nuclear war can fill a person with dread when they're focused on those effects.

- **Social relations**: Because of the devastation, people are going to do more to fit into a social setting. Something about a large-scale war would see people more likely to band together to maintain the social structure.

- **Decreased learning capacity and memory loss**: One symptom is forgetting things you learned. While it can start with things that you learned more recently, it can eventually affect things you knew before. The same applies to your memory. The trauma of the war can cause you to forget recent events, but it can just be the beginning. It is going to be more prevalent in those who were affected by radiation.

Chronic Reactions

The long-term psychological effects can still include the acute reactions, but there are some effects that are going to take longer to set in. These changes can be in how you express emotions, and they can even alter your entire personality. Remember that these can be intense reactions, or you might not have any reaction at all. There are a lot of factors that are going to be at play, and, again, these are just potential scenarios.

- **Psychoses**: Disorientation and hallucinations could be extremely common in a post-nuclear war world. Some individuals may even experience being in a catatonic state. This will likely be the first sign of neuroses that can set in later. However, it can remain prominent as the person attempts to grasp and process the reality of what just happened. This can be especially increased in those who witnessed any of the bombs falling.

- **Neuroses:** Neuroses can start with the acute reactions, or it can take place as the symptoms of psychoses subside. Weariness, lack of motivation, introverted tendencies, and memory loss will all be prevalent. These are also symptoms that can worsen over time.

- **Post-traumatic stress disorder (PTSD):** Soldiers engaged in long, intense battles and people who witness natural disasters up close will likely experience PTSD to some degree. In a nuclear war, while it is possible to feel this if you are in your shelter, it is more likely to affect you when you leave your shelter. The devastation of the area and the human casualties are going to immediately alter your psyche, especially when the reality of how helpless you are sets in. There are some signs of certainty if you or anyone around you might be dealing with PTSD, which include the following:

  o The affected person will have startled responses to everything, and they will be irritated at everything.

  o They will easily fly off the handle. This could be in place of startled responses or it can be the following emotion.

  o People suffering from PTSD seem to focus heavily on the scenario that caused the trauma.

  o They begin to close themselves off, which can seem like introversion in the beginning, but this would be much more severe.

  o The person seems to be in a strange dream-like state.

- The beginning stages are typically some of the hardest, but it's even tougher when you're trying to determine if it really is PTSD or acute reactions that a lot of the surviving population are going to have given they just lived through a nuclear war.

- **Phobias**: When nuclear war is long done, those who lived through it are going to be on edge because they are afraid that it could happen again. This anxiety is going to have the same appearance that other phobias do. Bright lights, thunderclaps, and even the subsequent weather after a nuclear war could all set off this response. Those who have read about radiation sickness could even have psychosomatic reactions, as they believe they have been affected by radiation.

- **Survivor's guilt**: Major traumatic events where there is a tremendous loss of life can make those who survived the ordeal feel guilty. This was something felt by the survivors of the atomic bombs in Japan, but perhaps the most common instance of it today in the US is from those who survived the attacks on September 11th. This can lead to manic depression, wherein the survivor will act more recklessly than before.

Again, the only real scale that we have for nuclear war is Japan, but you can still look to other events and examples throughout history. The war in the Middle East, September 11th, the Boston Marathon Bombing, survivors of mass shootings—there are plenty of examples of the psychological effects that would be worth knowing and trying to understand. There are going to be graphic and grim depictions of those events, so you need to understand why this knowledge is just as important as any first aid course.

After a large-scale nuclear war, we are without first responders and doctors, which includes therapists and counselors. You want to keep everyone alive, which means those psychological wounds are going to need treatment as well. Having an idea of what is going on and how to help will keep more people alive. This should also be knowledge that you pass on to someone else because it may be you who deals with trauma.

While you can't turn back the effects of psychological trauma, there are things that you can do to help someone who is suffering. By doing this, you will allow them the time to process what has happened, and you will ensure everyone else's safety.

- **Listen to them**: You should actively listen to the person as they describe what they feel. Try to engage them to get to the root of everything, but don't try to push the conversation in a certain way. Listen without judgment or trying to "fix" the problem. If you can do that, you will gain their trust, which will make them feel safe. The safer they feel in your care, the easier it will be for them to open up if they are experiencing any difficult emotions or feelings.

- **Let them have space**: This can be difficult if the person affected is a close loved one. You will have the instinct to hug them or touch them to show them they are safe, but this can put them more on edge. Let them reach out to you to let you know that physical touch is okay. Giving them space also applies to letting the conversation end when they are getting overwhelmed. Let them have a few moments to themselves. Check on them after, but don't try to bring the previous conversation back up.

    o If they are trying to apologize, accept it and move on. Do not hold on to this and try to bring it up later, and do not let them feel ashamed of needing that space.

- **Be attentive**: By making yourself present to them, you should start identifying when that person is being affected. After you have built a level of trust, then you can offer to point out things you notice that they do when they are triggered. Doing this will help them gain the ability to point out their own triggers and responses—making things operate more smoothly.

- **Be patient**: A person suffering from psychological effects is not going to know what they need or how to express their anguish—especially in the beginning. You can't get frustrated with them or try to force any other feelings on them.

- **Help them out with tasks**: This can be tricky. If you ask for too much, they can become easily overwhelmed. If you try to take everything away from them, they can start to feel useless, which can lead to depression. So, let the person keep the tasks you give them to help out, and if they are struggling to focus on a task (a symptom of PTSD), then you can step in and help out.

- **Find self-care practices**: Self-care is going to be difficult when in a sheltering situation or living in a post-apocalyptic world. However, there should still be self-care practices in place. This is where it's important to have books or board games on hand, and you should remember that not every waking moment needs to be about survival. There needs to be some breaks in the routine if you are not in a dire emergency.

When you think about the world after nuclear war, a lot of these practices need to be followed for everyone, yourself included. Even if you follow everything in the next section about prevention, you could still end up with some psychological trauma.

Can These Effects Be Prevented?

Eliminating all psychological trauma is going to be impossible. But there may be things that you can do ahead of time to reduce those effects. The first of these is going to be through preparedness and practice. Having an idea of what to expect can eliminate the "surprise" factor that can bring on that trauma.

Throughout this book, you are preparing yourself, which means any traumatic effects you feel might be reduced significantly. But now you need to pass that information down to the other people in your shelter, which can be a tough task, especially when you're having to explain it to your children. Even if they're old enough to understand, it's still going to be difficult for you.

However, the best way to inform them is to be as honest, easy to understand, and accurate as you can possibly be. First, you want to be real. Everyone around you is going to need to know what the nuclear war is going to look like, and they should know what the world afterward is going to be like. This is to prevent the psychological shock that can take place. Remember that being honest does not mean that you need to be overly detailed. Keep everything as simple as possible without losing any information.

Once you've given everyone an easy-to-understand and honest assessment of what nuclear war is going to look like and how it will impact your collective lives, you then need to give them an accurate assessment of that threat. For instance, you don't want your children to be paranoid about nuclear war when you know that diplomacy and cooler heads are doing what they can to avoid it. But you don't want to lie to them and tell them that there isn't an imminent threat. Let them know that it can happen, and make sure they understand if you are in an area that could be a target.

Remember that even if you are not in an area where the bombs are an immediate threat, they should still have accurate information about nuclear fallout and the other effects.

Psychological casualties are going to happen, and they will likely affect someone in your shelter, but knowing what to expect can make a world of difference when everyone should be banding together to ensure survival.

Maintaining PMA

I spent some time in *New Prepper's Survival Bible* discussing the importance of having a positive mental attitude (PMA), and how to get to that place of PMA. But what happens when you are faced with adversity, like in a post-nuclear world? It is extremely easy to lose sight of that positivity, so how can someone maintain PMA in a situation like this?

- **Have gratitude**: This is going to be the hardest thing to do after something like a nuclear war, but you have to take the small wins. So, each day (if you are able to), write down a few things that you are grateful for. Whether it's being safe and alive in your shelter or that you had some of your favorite snack food that day—these are things you can focus on, especially when you are facing what is beyond the walls of your shelter.

- **Do just a little more**: One thing that you can do to build positivity is pushing your boundaries little by little each day. Doing this shows you that you are skilled and capable of survival, and when you are faced with something a bit more difficult, you will have a better mindset to face it.

- **More positive words**: It's extremely difficult to say anything positive after a disaster. The world as you knew it is gone, which only fills you with negative feelings that turn into negative words. Feeling upset and down is okay, but you should make a conscious effort to speak words of positivity.

- **Encourage positivity**: Positivity is easy to achieve when you can encourage the other people around you to be positive, too. This can help everyone take the tasks of surviving and rebuilding in stride. It can even help you by just bringing someone's spirits up. The more positivity that goes around, the easier survival will be.

- **Meditate**: This is a form of self-care that can help you deal with the traumatic effects of a disaster while bringing yourself to a positive frame of mind. Even if you can't feel all the positive effects, it at least gives you a chance to not focus on anything except yourself.

- **Be realistic about results**: Just because you are tackling your tasks with a positive mindset doesn't mean that you will see results. Some things might fail, or there will just be no progress seen for quite some time. So, the best thing to do in this world is work toward what you're wanting while accepting that things aren't going to go in your favor.

Defense and Security

Once you are able to start leaving the shelter, you want to look for usable resources and determine if the area is worth rebuilding. You should also be thinking about the security and defense of that area. When you rebuild an area, it will be noticeable, which means you could be noticed by the wrong type of people.

Security

Now, when you start making a security plan, you want to work in layers. The more layers that you have, the more secure you can be and the more control you can have over a situation. With these layers themselves, you should think of them like the rings around a bullseye—where the center is directly over your home. When you rebuild a larger area or establish a community, you can teach everyone the same system.

Keep in mind that when you start establishing a community, it's best to keep it small. Rebuild in a small circle and expand outward. This will allow you to establish and maintain security around the entire perimeter.

- **Layer 1: Your neighborhood**: You should know your neighborhood in and out. The houses around you, roads, alleys, and everything else need to be accounted for when you explore outside your shelter. It's also helpful to learn who lives in those houses now. This can help you determine who is safe to approach and who you should take caution with.

- **Layer 2: Your property**: This is where you want to start putting in security measures. If you are able to monitor the outside of the shelter or your home, you want to ensure that there are no trees or bushes that can obstruct your views. Without electricity, you won't be able to get use of a home security system like cameras, but you can install some primitive noise traps. The closer you get to where your family is, the more you can start installing things like traps or tripwires.

- **Layer 3: Entrances**: While you want all the entry points to be secure for nuclear fallout, you want to make sure that they also discourage potential intruders. You also want to continue following security practices while inside the shelter. Make sure you lock doors and ensure that other potential entry points are secure.

- **Layer 4: Your shelter**: If your shelter is inside your home structure, then this will be split into two separate layers: your home and your shelter. If your home is an additional layer, you should consider hiding weapons that you can access easily in case someone does get past all your other layers of security. Inside the shelter itself, you want to make sure that the shelter is resistant to fire or chemical attacks. There should also be an escape route, in the event you encounter a worst-case scenario.

Defensive Methods

I've already gone over some of the types of weapons that you can have to keep you and your family safe. However, weapons alone aren't enough. You need a variety of strategies because not every attacker is going to be the same. This also accounts for the time when you run out of ammunition or don't have a gun at all. Remember, this is going to be a time of lawlessness, so you need every advantage you can get.

- **Don't be afraid to fight dirty**: Remember, there are no laws and no "codes of honor" here. Being engaged by an attacker here is a matter of life and death. Find the easiest weaknesses like their eyes or even their groin. Scratch, bite, and inflict as much pain as you can. Keep in mind that you can't really show mercy here to avoid a sneak attack. The person should be debilitated enough to give you plenty of time to escape.

- **Keep moving if there are multiple attackers**: While it makes for great action movie sequences, standing in the middle while being circled by attackers is not a great idea. They are not going to attack one at a time, so you need to start moving. Strike and run. Even if you do get someone to the ground, leave them to avoid a larger assault.

- **Use your weapons**: If you have weapons, use them. You want to inflict as much damage on an attacker as you can, so there should be no reason to leave weapons behind any time you go exploring. Knowing your weapon's limits and capabilities will help you make strategic strikes on an enemy. Your first strike should be to disarm them from their weapons. The following strikes should incapacitate them.

- **Take self-defense classes now**: Much like your first aid courses, you should find classes in self-defense. Martial arts, Krav Maga, Brazilian jiu jitsu, and even MMA training can help you in survival situations. If you have firearms, then you should take basic firearms courses. It may not seem like a lot, but you will be able to take strategic shots, which will save ammunition.

Establishing a New Community

Self-survival is important, but eventually, it is going to be time to establish connections with other survivors to start rebuilding society. This final section will go over all the things that you can do that can contribute to the continuation of humanity.

Survive the Aftermath

Surviving the attacks is going to be one step, but you also have to make sure you survive what waits on the other side. You are now dealing with a world that lacks all the comforts you are used to. You have to survive in a world without medicine, clean water, police, and doctors. Therefore, your initial goal is to keep yourself alive and learn how to adapt to this new world.

Scavenge for Supplies

When you are exploring the area, eventually you will start turning these trips out into scavenging missions. Even if you have a shelter stockpile, you want to make sure that there are enough immediate supplies available until the community is fully operational.

Look for food, medicine, ammunition, clothes, blankets, and anything that will be useful to people later on. There won't be space in your shelter for these things, so where will you store them? You can use your garage or the rooms in your home, which can eventually become the supply hub for the community.

Rebuild the Calendar

Eventually, you want to start thinking about planting and harvesting, which means you need a calendar. If you have kept up with the days while you are sheltering, then you will have a head start, but trying to establish a calendar in a post-nuclear world is going to be difficult. There are new weather patterns, and there is a screen between the ground and the sun, and you can't forget any radioactive contamination. This is going to take you a while, but you will need to find when the best time of year is for growing.

A calendar is also going to be helpful when it comes to knowing what supplies you're going to need and what you are going to use more of. For example, you would worry more about a firewood supply in the winter, so you can plan ahead to build a sufficient supply.

Food and Water

Establishing a new community means that everyone is going to need to have water and food, and that means having more than what you have in storage.

When it comes to food, you need to try to grow something in a garden as soon as possible. You want to be able to have a supply for everyone to eat, but you also want to account for the limited growing and individuals who may come to steal from your crops. The less you have to tap into reserves, the better off you will be.

The best option for water is a centralized well in the beginning. You could build wells in other places, too, but keep in mind that this is going to take a lot of digging to finally tap into a water source that isn't contaminated by radiation. Also, having a centralized well will make sure that everyone only gets what they need.

Reestablish Contact

You will have to be careful when trying to send the message out that you are establishing a new community. This will require you to find out the best way to send and receive messages, to which I would recommend a message drop-off point. This will allow you to establish contact and have meetings with a person or group of people before leading them to the community. If you are leading someone new to the community, you need to be careful. Watch all areas around you to make sure they are not part of a dangerous group.

You also don't want to refuse messages from an already established community. There's a chance they have made more significant progress than you, and it would be much simpler for you to move to that community. Any supplies you have gathered can be picked up on a group excursion.

While you have done everything to survive a nuclear war and the aftermath, you have to remember that other people have survived as well. Banding together is the best chance that humanity has. After finding or establishing a community, though, you want to put people in the places where they will benefit the community.

You are going to find even more strength in a group if everyone has a shared goal. That's not to say that there won't be individual ideas, but you don't want the group splintering because of those ideas. When you establish a community, establish goals for it that everyone can agree on. Getting something established can be tricky on its own, but there are other things that need to be implemented as soon as possible.

Protection

Once you establish the community, you need to put some kind of security in place. Take your layering plan and work outward. Make sure everyone in the community has some type of self-defense training, and teach them how to safely and effectively use a variety of weapons.

This is where condensing the group will make the most sense. Instead of spreading out through one neighborhood, perhaps you take up one or two blocks. This will allow you to establish a perimeter that will be monitored more efficiently. After you establish the perimeter, then start working on escape routes for everyone in the community. This will get everyone out and to safety in the event there is an ambush from a hostile group.

Establish Fair Laws

After the community and your goals are established, it would be beneficial to also make a set of laws for the community. While there shouldn't be issues, you can't rule out the possibility. What happens to someone who endangers the community? How will you handle someone who steals supplies? What happens in the event you neutralize an attacker? Everyone in the community should be aware of—and agree—to these rules. As a community leader, you should make sure that the rules are fair with no exceptions.

Share Knowledge

There may be some in the community who take the same approach as you, and there may be some that got there a different way. This means that there is a lot of knowledge to share. Not only would you want to know other survival methods, but you can also determine what everyone adds to the community. There will be those who are experts in firearms, and you might have some who can grow food with limited resources. Everyone involved should be willing to document this knowledge and start passing it onto the other people in the group.

As your community progresses, you won't just be a group of survivors. This will become a community that resembles what you are familiar with already. But remember that, eventually, you will want to explore other areas to establish contact with more communities. This will open up trading and bartering, which will expand further until we have reconnected the nation.

Rebuilding the world is going to take a long time, and, realistically, it might take several generations before one community connects with another. The important thing is to treat the rebuilding process as you would your first trips out of the shelter. Take things slow, and don't get frustrated when things seem to be barely progressing. Humanity will recover, and part of that will be because of the work that you start now.

Chapter 6:

The Future of Nuclear Weapons

In our new age of terrifying, lethal gadgets, which supplanted so swiftly the old one, the first great aggressive war, if it should come, will be launched by suicidal little madmen pressing and electronic button. Such a war will not last long and none will even follow it. There will be no conquerors and no conquests, but only the charred bones of the dead on an uninhabited planet. –William L. Shirer, The Rise and Fall of the Third Reich: A History of Nazi Germany

Nuclear technology and warfare advance as time moves on—it's a given. That's how warfare has worked since the first time humans engaged in conflict with other humans. But what makes the future of these weapons and this type of warfare so terrifying is how we will never know just how far those advancements go. When we are finally aware of their state, it is likely going to be too late.

Preparing for the Future NOW

While you can never accurately pinpoint what world leaders are going to do or what type of weapons exist, you should still be in a state of preparedness. Even after talks of nuclear war fade out of the news and social media, you should still be getting ready. Staying prepared can be as simple as going out to your shelter once a month and ensuring that everything is in working order. Staying prepared is maintaining your family's emergency kits every four months, and staying prepared is practicing emergency drills regularly.

Another thing you can do now to prepare for later is to start budgeting and stocking up on items that can be used as currency. You should have at least a small collection of precious metals like gold, silver, and platinum, but you should have extra medical supplies, alcohol (i.e. vodka, whiskey, and others), iodine tablets, toilet paper, and even bullets. As humanity starts to rebuild, use your stockpiles of food and medicine. After enough time, start bartering with the alcohol and ammunition. Then, once a community is established, you can use your precious metals.

Again, we are likely going to be in the dark about a nuclear attack until it's already on the way. But you can stay up-to-date with healthy research. Reputable podcasts, news outlets, books, and people around you can all offer some insight into what the current state of events is. Again, this should be done in a healthy way. When trying to speculate about how close we are to nuclear warfare, it can lead you down a rabbit hole of conspiracies and people trying to claim that certain things are real.

The Politics and Diplomacy of Nuclear Weapons Today

I did go over nuclear diplomacy, but you should keep in mind that these things can change rapidly. While the United States and several European countries struggle with the diplomatic breakdowns brought on by the war in Ukraine, they've also had to turn their sights on the growing tensions in China and the issues between North and South Korea. At the time of writing (May 2023), there are new tensions with Iran, as well.

Britain, France, and Germany have all threatened sanctions against Iran if they find that the country is enriching uranium to the levels needed for a nuclear weapon. Things started to come to a head when United Nations' inspectors found uranium particles at just above 80% purity coming from an underground nuclear facility. For clarity, bomb-grade uranium needs to reach 90% purity, and the Iranian facility is built underground, which protects it from air strikes. This makes things difficult for all countries involved. Talks with one country could upset an ally, which can lead to breakdowns of diplomacy between allies.

One of the things you should perform periodic checks on are diplomatic relations between countries. This will give you a good idea of what may be on the horizon.

The Role of Science and Technology in Nuclear Weapons Today

In 1983, the Soviet Union and the United States were still engaged in the Cold War. While there hadn't been another event like the Cuban Missile Crisis at this point, both countries were still on high alert as they tried to make advancements not only in their weapons but in their weapon detection technologies.

One night, Stanislav Petrov was working in a secret Soviet bunker outside the Russian capital of Moscow. Petrov had been assigned a simple task—watch satellite data and confirm any readings of a potential American attack. While things had been relatively quiet, one night, Petrov received an alert from the equipment. It was telling him that the US had launched a nuclear missile toward the Soviet Union.

Duty officers were also informed of the missile launch but needed confirmation from Petrov. Petrov's instincts were that this was a false alarm. The Soviet Union had been so desperate to make an advanced weapons detection system that they rushed through things and failed to give the system any sort of calibration. Because of that, Petrov knew there were going to be glitches in the system.

However, as he told duty officers that there was no missile on the way, there was another alert, followed by another. Before long, there were two more alerts that said the Americans were attacking. Duty officers were also informed of the five missiles on their way toward them; Petrov had to think and act quickly.

While he was on the phone with his duty officers, Petrov was also talking with technicians about the readings. He wanted some type of confirmation about a missile launch because something seemed off to him. Petrov wanted to know why there were only five missiles on the way. It was a foolish move to launch so little when the Soviets had more that they could counter with.

Those technicians were looking with their other radar systems, and they would even check their telescopes, but they reported nothing. There was nothing in the sky, which meant that Petrov, again, had to rely on his instincts.

Petrov was doing his best to keep his duty officers from authorizing a counterattack while the technicians got to the bottom of the alerts. Finally, they came back with a report that what the system read as nuclear missiles was actually sunlight that reflected off the tops of clouds. A computer system that had been designed to detect missiles much earlier had given false warnings that could have altered the course of history. There was almost a large-scale nuclear war, but because Petrov followed his instincts, he saved the world from destruction.

Now, let's look at the technological advancements that we have today. The 1990s were a period where technology advanced at a rapid rate, kicking off the talks about "smart machines." Artificial intelligence (AI) looks to be integrated in all aspects of our lives. It exists on social media, in our music apps, and on almost every device that is in our homes.

Some of these AI systems are extremely simplistic. They can turn our lights on and off, tell us the time and weather, or they can call family members after a series of voice commands. However, others are handling complex problems. It's a marvel because they are handling problems in seconds that can take a person significantly longer to complete. These intelligence systems then share information with each other. They begin to learn and adapt in an instant, but it is still an intelligence that needs work.

Look at the mistakes that AI can make; yet it is still being developed and implemented. What happens if this artificial intelligence comes in contact with the systems that control nuclear warheads? This is going to entice governments because they will feel like their country can react well in advance to a nuclear assault.

What happens if that AI detects sunlight but sends data that there are missiles coming? A country could immediately launch a counterattack, which would trigger a large-scale nuclear war. Or what if these AI systems "talk" to each other, which ends up spawning a war? We are also in the age of cyberattacks. An entire country's security could be compromised, which turns this breakthrough in technology into one of the worst blunders of mankind.

A Call to Action for Nuclear Preparedness

We have no control over nuclear weapons. We could hope to talk world leaders down and have them dismantle their nuclear armament, but it won't happen. Nuclear warfare is still something that is going to be researched and developed. As we advance technologically, so will our weapons. And for every weapon that one country assembles, there is a weapon being made by another country—ready to be used in a counterattack.

Much like all the natural disasters we face today, there is no way we can tell when or where a nuclear attack will happen. There is also no way to know why these weapons will get used. The only ones who will know that are the world leaders who have the ability to "push the big red button." This is why it is imperative that we treat this as a disaster situation and be prepared for it now.

Some people may ask why you are adamant about preparing for a nuclear attack—they'll simply argue that it will never happen. But do we not have fire drills despite there being no fires? We should be prepared for anything, including nuclear warfare. We have to prepare now, and if we never have to put these plans into action—good. We might not use our nuclear war preparedness, but what about our children or future generations? Having this knowledge now allows us to take it and pass it along for later use.

Starting with this book, and following all of your future prepping endeavors, you want to develop a set of survival skills that you will be able to teach others. These teachings will be preserved and carried on, which will create a system of education on these survival skills. That is why it is imperative that you start these preparations now.

Conclusion

The world was changed forever when "the gadget" was tested over the White Sands of New Mexico. Those developments led to one of the two most devastating attacks in history, and the development of nuclear bombs hasn't slowed down at all. Countries that were once prohibited from building weapons are showing signs of getting all the pieces together to build their own nuclear arsenal. And countries that already had access to nuclear weapons are threatening to use those weapons at a moment's notice. That leaves us with limited information aside from how awful it will be when the world enters a large-scale war.

It is a grim scenario because even a small-scale war can have devastating effects that will be felt across the globe. That's why it is so imperative to start work on things like building your shelter and stockpiling your supplies. It's also a great idea to take self-defense, firearms, and first aid classes. Knowing these things and having a stockpile of supplies will make you irreplaceable when it comes to rebuilding our world.

But while you are doing these things, you should also learn more about nuclear weapons and their effects. Where are they going to drop that's near you? Has diplomacy prevailed, or is it still deteriorating? Paying attention now will keep you alert for what may come. It's also extremely important to pass this knowledge along to other people. The more lives that we can save now, the better our chances will be of rebuilding the world in a post apocalyptic era.

If you know anyone who is wanting to make a preparedness plan for a nuclear war or other disasters, let them know that they can start with the *New Prepper Survival Bible* and work their way to this book. Afterward, you can share what you've learned along your own prepper journey, and you can learn things from them, too. If we all work together, we can survive.

As an independent author with a small marketing budget, reviews are my livelihood on this platform. I would be incredibly thankful if you could take just 60 seconds to write a brief review on Amazon, even if it's just a few sentences! You can do so by scanning the QR code below. I love hearing from my readers, and personally read every single review.

Scan the QR code below!

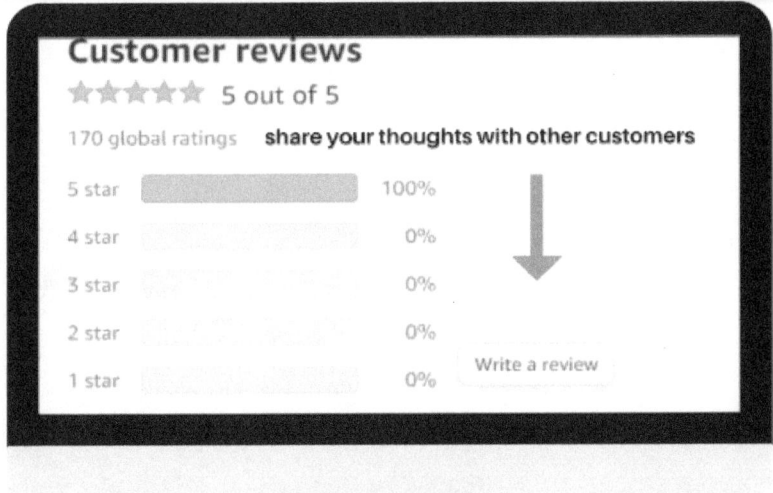

SCAN ME

JUST FOR YOU!

As a way of saying **THANK YOU** for your purchase, I'm offering you these **2 FREE** bonus gifts exclusive to my readers!

FREE bonus #1: 10 Essential Home Remedy Supplies For Preppers

FREE bonus #2: 20 Hygiene Products That All Preppers Should Store

To receive your 2 FREE bonus gifts scan the QR code below:

SCAN ME

References

Adrian, S. (2018, February 20). *How to build an earthbag house (and why you should)*. Off Grid World. https://offgridworld.com/build-earthbag-house/

Albert Einstein Quotes. (n.d.). *Albert Einstein quotes*. BrainyQuote. Retrieved April 25, 2023, from https://www.brainyquote.com/quotes/albert_einstein_122873

American Red Cross. (2018). *Disaster Preparedness Plan*. Redcross.org. https://www.redcross.org/get-help/how-to-prepare-for-emergencies/make-a-plan.html

Associated Press. (2022, October 25). *What is a dirty bomb, and how dangerous is it?* The Guardian. https://www.theguardian.com/world/2022/oct/25/what-is-a-dirty-bomb-and-how-dangerous-is-it

The BBC. (2018, July 16). *US nuclear materials stolen last year are still missing*. BBC News. https://www.bbc.com/news/world-us-canada-44852863

CDC. (2020a, February 24). *Making water safe in an emergency*. Centers for Disease Control and Prevention. https://www.cdc.gov/healthywater/emergency/making-water-safe.html

CDC. (2020b, October 22). *Preventing and treating radiation injuries and illness*. Www.cdc.gov. https://www.cdc.gov/nceh/radiation/emergencies/symptoms.htm

Contributor, G. (2017, November 18). *Why geodesic shelters make the best emergency shelters*. The Prepper Journal.

https://theprepperjournal.com/2017/11/18/geodesic-shelters-make-best-emergency-shelters/

Dartnell, L. (2014, April 16). *A 7-step guide for rebooting civilization after the apocalypse*. Time. https://time.com/62074/a-7-step-guide-for-rebooting-civilization-after-the-apocalypse/

Dexter Gordon Quotes. (n.d.). *Dexter Gordon Quotes*. BrainyQuote. Retrieved May 4, 2023, from https://www.brainyquote.com/quotes/dexter_gordon_197934

Duff, B. (2022, January 7). *Here's the essential SHTF survival gear you need.* Mind4Survival. https://mind4survival.com/shtf-gear/

Federation of American Scientists. (2022). *Status of world nuclear forces.* Federation of American Scientists. https://fas.org/issues/nuclear-weapons/status-world-nuclear-forces/

Freedman, L. D. (n.d.). *Strategic Arms Reduction Talks - START III/SORT*. Encyclopedia Britannica. Retrieved April 21, 2023, from https://www.britannica.com/event/Strategic-Arms-Reduction-Talks/START-III-SORT

G, J. r. (2020, March 19). *Prepper home security: stay safe now & during a disaster.* DIY Prepper. https://www.diyprepper.com/prepper-home-security/

Gooden, M. (2022, January 28). *How to help someone with trauma: what to say and do.* Psych Central. https://psychcentral.com/health/how-to-help-someone-with-trauma#what-to-say-and-avoid

Henry, P. (2021, March 3). *How to stock a survival pantry.* The Prepper Journal. https://theprepperjournal.com/2021/03/03/how-to-stock-a-survival-pantry/

Hickok, K. (2018, November 5). *After a zombie apocalypse, here are 9 keys to rebuilding a civilization.* Livescience.com. https://www.livescience.com/64011-rebuild-civilization-post-zombie-apocalypse.html

History.com Editors. (2009, October 27). *Cold War history.* History. https://www.history.com/topics/cold-war/cold-war-history

History.com Editors. (2017, July 26). *Manhattan Project.* History. https://www.history.com/topics/world-war-ii/the-manhattan-project

History.com Editors. (2022, July 25). *Bombing of Hiroshima and Nagasaki.* History. https://www.history.com/topics/world-war-ii/bombing-of-hiroshima-and-nagasaki

Hunter, J. (2015, October 18). *The 7 different types of weapons - which should you choose?* Primal Survivor. https://www.primalsurvivor.net/types-of-weapons/

Indeed Editorial Team. (2023, February 3). *10 tips for maintaining a Positive Attitude.* Indeed Career Guide. https://www.indeed.com/career-advice/career-development/how-to-keep-a-positive-attitude

Isachenkov, V. (2023, February 21). *Russia suspends only remaining major nuclear treaty with US.* ABC News. https://abcnews.go.com/International/wireStory/putin-suspends-russias-involvement-key-nuclear-arms-pact-97350404

Kearny, C. H. (1979, September). *Ch. 8: Water - Nuclear War Survival Skills.* Www.oism.org. https://www.oism.org/nwss/s73p919.htm

Kevin Costner Quotes. (n.d.). *Kevin Costner quotes.* BrainyQuote. Retrieved May 3, 2023, from https://www.brainyquote.com/quotes/kevin_costner_267030

Kylene. (n.d.). *How to store water for emergency preparedness.* The Provident Prepper. https://theprovidentprepper.org/how-to-store-water-for-emergency-preparedness/

Lockie, A. (2022, December 26). *Russia threatened to vaporize US cities — here are the areas in the US most likely to be hit in a nuclear attack.* Business Insider. https://www.businessinsider.com/likely-us-nuclear-targets-2017-5

Malcolm Gladwell Quotes. (n.d.). *The Bomber Mafia Quotes by Malcolm Gladwell.* Www.goodreads.com. Retrieved May 1, 2023, from https://www.goodreads.com/work/quotes/88566827-the-bomber-mafia-a-dream-a-temptation-and-the-longest-night-of-the-se

Martindale, M. (2021, July 30). *Michigan-bound radioactive material reported missing has been recovered.* The Detroit News. https://www.detroitnews.com/story/news/local/michigan/20 21/07/30/michigan-bound-radioactive-material-reported-missing-has-been-recovered/5430232001/

MasterClass. (2021, July 15). *Ultimate bug-out bag guide: survival kit checklist.* Master Class. https://www.masterclass.com/articles/bug-out-bag-list

Mickley, G. A. (n.d.). *Psychological factors in nuclear warfare.* Retrieved May 8, 2023, from https://ke.army.mil/bordeninstitute/published_volumes/nucle arwarfare/chapter8/chapter8.pdf

Mitsanas, M. (2023, April 25). *South Korea considers the nuclear option as external threats mount.* NBC News. https://www.nbcnews.com/news/world/south-korea-north-nuclear-options-united-states-ballistic-missiles-rcna81171

Murphy, R. (2023, March 27). *8 signs that nuclear war is imminent.* Urban Survival Site. https://urbansurvivalsite.com/signs-nuclear-war-is-imminent/

Northwest Shelter Systems. (n.d.). *Underground bomb shelter emergency supplies for survival.* Northwest Shelter Systems. https://www.northwestsheltersystems.com/resources/bomb-shelter-supplies/

Office of Nuclear Energy. (2021, April 1). *Fission and fusion: what is the difference?* U.S. Department of Energy. https://www.energy.gov/ne/articles/fission-and-fusion-what-difference

Office of the Historian. (n.d.). *Foreign Relations of the United States, 1961–1963, Volume VI, Kennedy-Khrushchev Exchanges.* History.state.gov. https://history.state.gov/historicaldocuments/frus1961-63v06/d65

Oliver, M. (2017, June 23). *10 brutal realities of life after the nuclear apocalypse.* Listverse. https://listverse.com/2017/06/23/10-brutal-realities-of-life-after-the-nuclear-apocalypse/

The Preparedness Experience. (2022, March 29). *The ultimate prepper first aid kit.* The Preparedness Experience. https://thepreparednessexperience.com/prepper-first-aid-kit/

Prepper, C. V. (2018, April 6). *9 ways to DIY a low effort & cheap bomb shelter.* Survivopedia. https://www.survivopedia.com/9-ways-to-diy-a-low-effort-cheap-bomb-shelter/

RAND Corporation. (2018, April 23). *How artificial intelligence could increase the risk of nuclear war.* Www.rand.org. https://www.rand.org/blog/articles/2018/04/how-artificial-intelligence-could-increase-the-risk.html

REMM. (2017). *8 categories of radiation dosimeters for dose and exposure monitoring and worker safety.* Hhs.gov. https://remm.hhs.gov/radiation-dosimeters-dose-monitoring-worker-safety.htm

Reuters. (2023, May 5). *Smoldering Iran nuclear crisis risks catching fire.* US News. https://www.usnews.com/news/world/articles/2023-05-05/analysis-smoldering-iran-nuclear-crisis-risks-catching-fire

Suciu, P. (2021, March 12). *The U.S. Military is missing six nuclear weapons.* The National Interest. https://nationalinterest.org/blog/reboot/us-military-missing-six-nuclear-weapons-180032

Sultan, D. A. (2021, June 5). *India's Nuclear black market.* Strafasia | Strategy, Analysis, News and Insight of Emerging Asia. https://strafasia.com/indias-nuclear-black-market/

Urban, A. (2016, July 26). 6 self-defense tips for urban survivalists. Urban Survival Site. https://urbansurvivalsite.com/6-self-defense-tips-urban-survivalists/

Vendantu. (n.d.). *Nuclear winter.* VEDANTU. Retrieved May 3, 2023, from https://www.vedantu.com/biology/nuclear-winter

Wandia, M. (2021, April 2). *US nuclear target list - and safest locations to consider (2021-Updated).* TheSurvivalGeek.com. https://thesurvivalgeek.com/us-nuclear-target-list/

Wikipedia Contributors. (n.d.-a). *Nuclear triad.* Wikipedia. Retrieved April 24, 2023, from https://en.wikipedia.org/wiki/Nuclear_triad

Wikipedia Contributors. (n.d.-b). *Nuclear weapon.* Wikipedia. Retrieved April 21, 2023, from https://en.wikipedia.org/wiki/Nuclear_weapon

Wikipedia Contributors. (n.d.-c). *Treaty on the Prohibition of Nuclear Weapons.* Wikipedia. Retrieved April 21, 2023, from https://en.wikipedia.org/wiki/Treaty_on_the_Prohibition_of_Nuclear_Weapons

Wikipedia Contributors. (n.d.-d). *Tsar Bomba.* Wikipedia. Retrieved April 20, 2023, from https://en.wikipedia.org/wiki/Tsar_Bomba

Wolfson, R., & Dalnoki-Veress, F. (2022, March 2). *The devastating effects of nuclear weapons.* The MIT Press Reader. https://thereader.mitpress.mit.edu/devastating-effects-of-nuclear-weapons-war/

Image References

abietams. (2017, July 24). *Walkie talkie handheld transceiver [Image]*. Pixabay. https://pixabay.com/photos/walkie-talkie-handheld-transceiver-2534576/

TheDigitalArtist. (2017, July 27). *Armageddon destruction apocalypse [Image]*. Pixabay. https://pixabay.com/photos/armageddon-destruction-apocalypse-2546068/

Gigglekid. (2014, September 2). *Vulcan bomber aircraft aeroplane [Image]*. Pixabay. https://pixabay.com/photos/vulcan-bomber-aircraft-aeroplane-429992/

hosny_salah. (2021, August 16). *Man evacuation disaster catastrophe [Image]*. Pixabay. https://pixabay.com/photos/man-evacuation-disaster-catastrophe-6543133/

kalhh. (2017, October 1). *Apocalypse end time war destruction [Image]*. Pixabay. https://pixabay.com/photos/apocalypse-end-time-war-destruction-2806679/

lenzius. (2107, October 10). *Fallout shelter nuclear fallout [Image]*. Pixabay. https://pixabay.com/photos/fallout-shelter-nuclear-fallout-2835496/

linn_stokke0. (2015, June 12). *Winter desolate white nature frost [Image]*. Pixabay. https://pixabay.com/photos/winter-desolate-white-nature-frost-805703/

TBIT. (2015, September 28). *Alarm light siren emergency [Image]*. Pixabay. https://pixabay.com/photos/alarm-light-siren-emergency-959592/

WikiImages. (2013, January 3). *Explosion mushroom cloud*. Pixabay. https://pixabay.com/photos/explosion-mushroom-cloud-67557/

www.ingramcontent.com/pod-product-compliance
Lightning Source LLC
Chambersburg PA
CBHW020411130626
46549CB00006B/2520